Guided
MATH
Workstations

6-8

The minimum height to ride Colossal Roller Coaster is 50 inches. Choose the correct inequality symbol to represent the situation. Show the inequality on the number line.

$h \geq 50$

Authors

Donna Boucher

Laney Sammons, M.L.S.

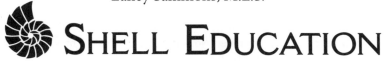

SHELL EDUCATION

For information on how this resource meets national and other state standards, see pages 13–14. You may also review this information by visiting our website at www.teachercreatedmaterials.com/administrators/correlations/ and following the on-screen directions.

Publishing Credits

Corinne Burton, M.A.Ed., *President*; Conni Medina, M.A.Ed., *Managing Editor*; Diana Kenney M.A.Ed., NBCT, *Content Director*; Veronique Bos, *Creative Director*; Robin Erickson, *Art Director*; Kristy Stark, M.A.Ed., *Editor;* Fabiola Sepulveda, *Graphic Designer;* Kyleena Harper, *Assistant Editor*

Image Credits

All images from iStock and Shutterstock.

Standards

Shell Education

A division of Teacher Created Materials
5301 Oceanus Drive
Huntington Beach, CA 92649-1030
http://www.tcmpub.com/shell-education
ISBN 978-1-4258-1730-5
©2018 Shell Educational Publishing, Inc.

Table of Contents

Introduction

GUIDE Workstation Tasks

G ames for **Mathematicians**

U sing What **We Know**

Table of Contents *(cont.)*

Independent Math Work

Developing Fluency

Expressing Mathematical Ideas

Appendix

The Guided Math Framework

Guided Math (Sammons 2010, 2014) is an instructional framework that helps teachers provide quality mathematics instruction for their students. Teachers address their students' varied learning needs within a carefully planned numeracy-rich environment where students are challenged to not just *do* math but instead *become* mathematicians. Implemented together, Guided Math's seven components are designed to help students as they develop a deep conceptual understanding of math, acquire computational fluency, and become skilled in thinking and acting mathematically.

Figure I.1 Instructional Components of Guided Math

Classroom Environment of Numeracy (Daily)
Students are immersed in a classroom environment that contains evidence of real-life math tasks, data analysis, math word walls, measuring tools, mathematical communication, class-created math anchor charts, graphic organizers, calendars, and authentic problem-solving challenges.
Math Warm-Ups (Daily)
This daily appetizer prepares students for "Your Choice" entrees with Math Stretches, calendar activities, problems of the day, reviews of skills to be maintained, and previews of skills to come.
Whole-Class Instruction (Your Choice)
Students are instructed as a whole group to activate prior knowledge, to model and think aloud, to read math-related literature aloud, to review and assess, or for Math Huddles.
Small-Group Instruction (Your Choice)
Students are instructed in small groups based on student needs to introduce new concepts, practice new skills, work with manipulatives, provide intensive and targeted instruction to struggling learners, provide additional challenge, introduce Math Workshop activities, and conduct informal assessments.
Math Workshop (Your Choice)
Students work independently, either individually, in pairs, or in groups, on tasks that may include extensions of other activities, mastered skills, investigations, math games, math journals, or interdisciplinary work, while teachers conduct small-group lessons and conferences.
Conferences (Daily)
Teachers confer with students to assess understanding, provide opportunities for math communication, determine instructional needs, and deliver brief teaching points.
Assessment (Daily)
Students are assessed through observation, on final work products, and during mathematical conversations. Assessment *for* learning and *of* learning are key to informing instruction.

(Sammons 2010)

What Is Math Workshop?

Math Workshop is a key ingredient of success in a Guided Math classroom (Sammons 2010, 2013). As one of the most versatile components of the framework, it accommodates a vast array of learning tasks. Not only does it provide opportunities for students to learn how to work independently on worthwhile mathematical endeavors, it also allows teachers to work with small groups or to confer with individual students.

During Math Workshop, students work independently—individually, in pairs, or in groups—and participate in Math Workstation tasks that have been designed to provide ongoing practice of previously mastered concepts and skills, to promote computational fluency, and to encourage mathematical curiosity and inquiry. In the first weeks of school, students learn and repeatedly practice the routines and procedures that make Math Workshop function smoothly. As students assume greater independence for their learning during Math Workshop, teachers may then expand their teaching roles.

Figure I.2 The Roles of Teachers and Students during Math Workshop

Teachers	Students
• Teach small-group lessons • Conduct math conferences • Informally assess learning through observations • Facilitate mathematical learning and curiosity through questioning	• Assume responsibility for their learning and behavior • Function as fledgling mathematicians • Communicate mathematically with peers • Review and practice previously mastered concepts and skills • Improve computational fluency • Increase ability to work cooperatively with peers

What Are Math Workstations?

Workstations are collections of tasks stored together and worked on independently of the teacher by students in specified workspaces. Students often work in pairs or small groups but may work alone. Each station contains a variety of carefully selected math tasks to support mathematical learning. Some of the tasks may be mandatory, while others may be optional. Essential for an effective Math Workshop is the inclusion of high-quality, appropriate tasks in the workstations. By grappling with these tasks independently, students gain greater mathematical proficiency and confidence in their mathematical abilities. Here, students "practice problem solving while reasoning, representing, communicating, and making connections among mathematical topics as the teacher observes and interacts with individuals at work or meets with a small group for differentiated math instruction" (Diller 2011, 7).

Math Centers versus Math Workstations

For many years, classrooms contained Math Centers where learners worked independently. Math Centers were considerably different from today's Math Workstations. Even the label *Math Workstation* clearly sends the message that students are expected to work as mathematicians. Workstation tasks are not included for fun alone but to further students' understanding of math, improve their computational fluency, and increase their mathematical competency. The chart below highlights the differences between Math Centers and Math Workstations.

Figure I.3 Math Centers versus Math Workstations

Math Centers	Math Workstations
• Games and activities are introduced to students when distributed at centers and are rarely used for instructional purposes.	• Tasks are derived from materials previously used during instruction, so students are already familiar with them.
• Centers are often thematic and change weekly.	• Tasks are changed for instructional purposes, not because it is the end of the week.
• Centers are often made available to students after they complete their regular work.	• Tasks provide ongoing practice to help students retain and deepen their understanding and are an important part of students' mathematical instruction.
• All students work on the same centers, and activities are seldom differentiated.	• Tasks are differentiated to meet the identified learning needs of students.

The GUIDE Model

The GUIDE model provides a simple and efficient organizational system for Math Workshop. With this model there are five Math Workstations, each with a menu of tasks from which students may work. The workstation tasks may be required, optional, or a combination of the two. You as the teacher decide which best meets the needs of your students. Instead of rotating from station to station, students work on only one station per day. By the end of a week, however, students will have worked at all five GUIDE stations.

The GUIDE acronym stands for the following:

Games for Mathematicians: Math games used to maintain previously mastered mathematical concepts and skills and promote computational proficiency

Using What We Know: Problem solving or challenge activities to draw upon mathematical understanding and skills

Independent Math Work: Materials used to teach previously mastered content incorporated into workstation tasks (paper-and-pencil tasks may be included)

Developing Fluency: Tasks that help students develop number sense and mental math skills

Expressing Mathematical Ideas: Tasks with opportunities to solidify mathematical vocabulary and encourage communication (math journals or math vocabulary notebooks may be included)

Students may be given the choice of where they will work each day, or the teacher may make team assignments. If you allow your students to choose their stations, provide a weekly checklist to track completed stations. Using the checklist, they will clearly see which stations they still need to complete by the end of the week.

This model offers maximum flexibility to teachers. Not only can the composition of small-group lessons be changed at a moment's notice to respond to newly identified student needs, but the length of the lessons may also vary from group to group. Teachers also appreciate another aspect of the flexibility this model offers. If the Math Workshop schedule is interrupted for some reason (e.g., testing day, holiday, whole-group lesson), the rotation schedule simply continues the next day as Math Workshop resumes. So, if a student does *G* on Monday, *U* on Tuesday, and then there is no workshop on Wednesday, he or she would do *I* on Thursday. As a result, students might not do all five workstations in one week, but they would still get to do them all after five Math Workshop days.

Differentiating Math Workstation Tasks

It is important that workstation tasks are differentiated to meet the unique needs of learners. Task Menus should clearly indicate which tasks have these options, and directions for these tasks should explain each of the options. Students need to know not only what the options are, but also which of them they should complete. Rather than labeling the options by ability level, various options for differentiation may be indicated by color, shape, or other symbol. For example, if there are three options, one might be coded with a circle, one with a triangle, and one with a square. Let students know which options they will complete by assigning them to the shape that best meets their learning needs.

While much focus has been placed on differentiation for struggling students, differentiation for those who may need extra challenge is equally important. There are several ways to provide differentiation. Tasks may be differentiated by:

- **Providing completely different tasks**—In some instances, students at one workstation will work on completely different tasks to address identified needs.

- **Providing variations of the same task**—This is the most efficient way to differentiate Math Workstation tasks because students work on the same task with some variations, so it can be introduced to everyone at the same time rather than having to introduce different tasks for different students. The task might be differentiated by changing the numbers, operations involved, or other aspects of the task to make it appropriate for all learners. Students who struggle with reading may require a recording of the task directions or other written materials. Some students may need to have manipulatives available. Others may benefit from having vocabulary cards with visual representations as references. Consider students' needs and offer support, if necessary, but use your professional judgment to avoid providing ongoing supports that become crutches rather than scaffolds for learning. Each task provided in this resource offers suggestions for differentiation to address individual students' needs.

- **Providing multiple ways for students to show their learning**—Students who struggle may benefit from the use of manipulatives to demonstrate their mathematical understanding. Students who need a challenge may create graphic organizers to display their work or graphs to represent data.

How to Use This Book

The tasks in this book have been designed for use with the GUIDE Workshop Model, but they may be incorporated into any workshop model you choose. It is important to model and practice these workstation tasks and the sentence stems on the *Talking Points* cards with students before expecting students to complete them independently.

Workstation Organization

An **overview** of the lesson, materials, objective, procedure, and differentiation is provided for the teacher on the first page of each GUIDE workstation task.

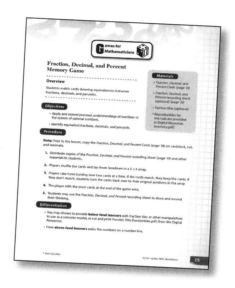

A **Student Task card** with directions and a materials list is provided for easy implementation and organization. Students may use the materials list as they put away their math workstation task so that all materials are included.

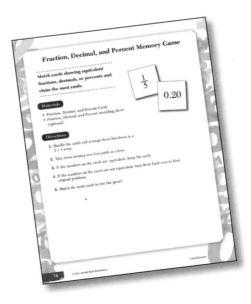

A **Talking Points card** with math vocabulary words and sentence stems is provided to encourage mathematical discourse. Consider copying it on brightly colored paper to draw students' attention. Laminate and store it with the student task card and other resources for each workstation task.

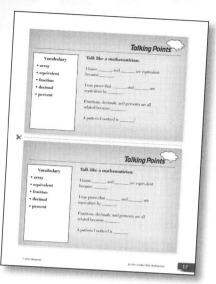

Additional **resources** for each task (e.g., spinners, cards, activity sheets) are included.

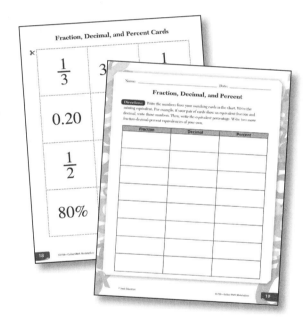

Digital resources to support the workstation tasks in this book are available online. A complete list of available documents is provided on pages 142. To access the digital resources, go to this website: **http://www.tcmpub.com/download-files**. Enter this code: 48385815. Follow the on-screen directions.

Introduction to Standards Correlations

Shell Educational Publishing is committed to producing educational materials that are research- and standards-based. In this effort, we have correlated all of our products to the academic standards of all 50 states, the District of Columbia, the Department of Defense Dependents Schools, and all Canadian provinces.

How to Find Standards Correlations

To print a customized correlation report of this product for your state, visit our website at **http://www.tcmpub.com/shell-education**. If you require assistance in printing correlation reports, please contact our Customer Service Department at 1-877-777-3450.

Purpose and Intent of Standards

The Every Student Succeeds Act (ESSA) mandates that all states adopt challenging academic standards that help students meet the goal of college and career readiness. While many states already adopted academic standards prior to ESSA, the act continues to hold states accountable for detailed and comprehensive standards.

Standards are designed to focus instruction and guide adoption of curricula. Standards are statements that describe the criteria necessary for students to meet specific academic goals. They define the knowledge, skills, and content students should acquire at each level. Standards are also used to develop standardized tests to evaluate students' academic progress.

Teachers are required to demonstrate how their lessons meet state standards. State standards are used in the development of all of our products, so educators can be assured they meet the academic requirements of each state.

The workstation tasks in this book are aligned to today's national and state-specific college-and-career readiness standards. The chart on pages 13–14 shows the correlation of those standards to the workstation tasks.

Standards Correlations

Workstation Task	College-and-Career Readiness Standard(s)
Fraction, Decimal, and Percent Memory Game (page 15)	Apply and extend previous understandings of numbers to the system of rational numbers. Identify equivalent fractions, decimals, and percents.
Difference from One (page 20)	Add, subtract, multiply, and divide using fractions with like and unlike denominators.
Dodge the Zombie (page 26)	Use facts about supplementary, complementary, vertical, and adjacent angles to solve simple equations for an unknown angle in a figure.
Integer Tug-of-War (page 32)	Apply and extend previous understandings of numbers to the system of rational numbers by adding and subtracting integers.
Exploring Manipulatives (page 37)	Make sense of problems and persevere in solving them.
Linking Cube Equations (page 40)	Apply and extend previous understandings of arithmetic to algebraic expressions.
What's the Point? (page 44)	Make sense of quantities and their relationships and justify decisions using words, numbers, and pictures.
Graphing Growing Patterns (page 52)	Apply and extend previous understandings of arithmetic to algebraic expressions.
You Write the Story (page 56)	Represent and solve problems involving addition and subtraction.
Express Yourself (page 62)	Use properties of operations to generate equivalent expressions.
Data Detective (page 73)	Display and summarize numerical data, give quantitative measures, and describe overall patterns.

Slope and Intercept (page 80)	Graph a line, determine the slope of the line, and derive the slope-intercept form.
Rate and Ratio Task Cards (page 86)	Solve real-world problems using ratio and rate reasoning.
Greatest Common Factor Bingo (page 94)	Find the greatest common factor (GCF) of two numbers less than or equal to 100. Use the distributive property to express a sum of two whole numbers 1–100 with a common factor as a multiple of a sum of two whole numbers with no common factor.
Integer Battle (page 106)	Understand that positive and negative numbers describe quantities having opposite values. Add and subtract positive and negative numbers.
Scientific Notation (page 111)	Use numbers expressed in the form of a single digit multiplied by an integer power of 10 to estimate very large or very small quantities. Perform operations with numbers expressed in scientific notation.
Making Connections (page 122)	Make sense of mathematics by formulating personal, mathematical, and real-world connections to mathematical concepts.
3-2-1 Learning Log (page 128)	Reflect on a math objective and precisely communicate mathematical thinking.
All About… (page 132)	Use precise mathematical language, numbers, and/or drawings to represent a mathematical concept.
Wanted Vocabulary Poster (page 135)	Use precise language to communicate mathematical ideas. Make connections between related mathematical concepts.

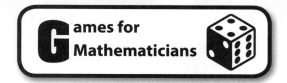

Fraction, Decimal, and Percent Memory Game

- -

Overview

Students match cards showing equivalencies between fractions, decimals, and percents.

- -

Materials

- *Fraction, Decimal, and Percent Cards* (page 18)

- *Fraction, Decimal, and Percent* recording sheet (optional) (page 19)

- fraction tiles (optional)

* The *Talking Points* card and these reproducibles are also provided in the Digital Resources (memory.pdf)

Objectives

- Apply and extend previous understandings of numbers to the system of rational numbers.

- Identify equivalent fractions, decimals, and percents.

Procedure

Note: Prior to the lesson, copy the *Fraction, Decimal, and Percent Cards* (page 18) on cardstock, cut, and laminate.

1. Distribute copies of the *Fraction, Decimal, and Percent* recording sheet (page 19) and other materials to students.

2. Players shuffle the cards and lay them facedown in a 3 × 4 array.

3. Players take turns turning over two cards at a time. If the cards match, they keep the cards. If they don't match, students turn the cards back over to their original positions in the array.

4. The player with the most cards at the end of the game wins.

5. Students may use the *Fraction, Decimal, and Percent* recording sheet to show and extend their thinking.

Differentiation

- You may choose to provide **below-level learners** with fraction tiles or other manipulatives to use as a concrete model, or print and cut *Fraction Tiles* (fractiontiles.pdf) from the Digital Resources.

- Have **above-level learners** order the numbers on a number line.

Fraction, Decimal, and Percent Memory Game

Match cards showing equivalent fractions, decimals, or percents and claim the most cards.

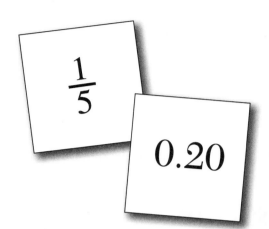

Materials

- *Fraction, Decimal, and Percent Cards*
- *Fraction, Decimal, and Percent* recording sheet (optional)

Directions

1. Shuffle the cards and arrange them facedown in a 3 × 4 array.

2. Take turns turning over two cards at a time.

3. If the numbers on the cards are equivalent, keep the cards.

4. If the numbers on the cards are not equivalent, turn them back over to their original positions.

5. Match the most cards to win the game!

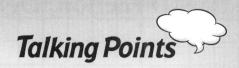

Talking Points

Vocabulary

- **array**
- **equivalent**
- **fraction**
- **decimal**
- **percent**

Talk like a mathematician:

I know _____ and _____ are equivalent because _____.

I can prove that _____ and _____ are equivalent by _____.

Fractions, decimals, and percents are all related because _____.

A pattern I noticed is _____.

Talking Points

Vocabulary

- **array**
- **equivalent**
- **fraction**
- **decimal**
- **percent**

Talk like a mathematician:

I know _____ and _____ are equivalent because _____.

I can prove that _____ and _____ are equivalent by _____.

Fractions, decimals, and percents are all related because _____.

A pattern I noticed is _____.

Fraction, Decimal, and Percent Cards

$\dfrac{1}{3}$	33%	$\dfrac{1}{5}$
0.20	$\dfrac{3}{4}$	75%
$\dfrac{1}{2}$	0.5	$\dfrac{4}{5}$
80%	$\dfrac{1}{20}$	0.05

Name: _____ Date: _____

Fraction, Decimal, and Percent

Directions: Write the numbers from your matching cards in the chart. Then, write the missing equivalent. Write two more fraction-decimal-percent equivalencies of your own.

Fraction	Decimal	Percent

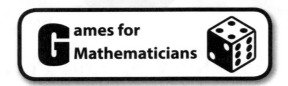

Difference from One

Overview

Students add, subtract, multiply, or divide four fractions in any combination to try to get the smallest difference from one.

Objective

Add, subtract, multiply, and divide fractions with like and unlike denominators.

Materials

- *Difference from One Fraction Cards* (pages 23–24)

- *Multiplication Chart* (optional) (page 25)

* The *Talking Points* card and these reproducibles are also provided in the Digital Resources (difference.pdf)

Procedure

Note: Prior to introducing the workstation, copy three to four sets of the *Difference from One Fraction Cards* (pages 23–24) on cardstock, laminate, and cut apart.

1. Players shuffle the cards and place them facedown in a draw pile.

2. Each player draws four cards and adds, subtracts, multiplies, or divides the fractions in any combination to get as close to one as possible.

3. Each player calculates his or her difference from one. The player with the smallest difference wins the round and earns one point. Players who reach one exactly earn two points. If the cards run out, reshuffle them and start over.

4. The player with the most points at the end of the game wins.

5. Students may document their results from each hand in their math journals.

Differentiation

- Allow **below-level learners** to use the *Multiplication Chart* (page 25) to find common denominators. For $\frac{1}{3}$, for example, read across the row marked 1 for the numerator and the row marked 3 for the denominator to find equivalent fractions.

- Challenge **above-level learners** by creating cards with improper fractions, mixed numbers, and/or whole numbers, in addition to proper fractions.

Difference from One

Add, subtract, multiply, and divide four fractions to get the smallest difference from one.

Materials

- *Difference from One Fraction Cards*

Directions

1. Shuffle the cards and place them facedown in a draw pile.

2. Each player draws four cards and adds, subtracts, multiplies, or divides the fractions in any combination to get as close to one as possible.

3. Each player calculates the difference between his or her result and one.

4. The player with the smallest difference earns one point. Players who reach one exactly earn two points. If the cards run out, reshuffle them and continue play.

5. The player with the most points at the end of play wins.

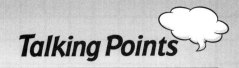

Talking Points

<table>
<tr>
<td>

Vocabulary

- **equivalent fraction**
- **numerator**
- **denominator**
- **common denominator**
- **product**
- **factors**
- **quotient**

</td>
<td>

Talk like a mathematician:

I have to find common denominators when adding or subtracting fractions because _____.

I can find common denominators by _____.

The product of two fractions is smaller than either of the factors because _____.

The quotient is not always smaller than the fractions being divided because _____.

</td>
</tr>
</table>

 -

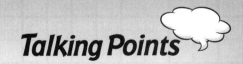

Talking Points

<table>
<tr>
<td>

Vocabulary

- **equivalent fraction**
- **numerator**
- **denominator**
- **common denominator**
- **product**
- **factors**
- **quotient**

</td>
<td>

Talk like a mathematician:

I have to find common denominators when adding or subtracting fractions because _____.

I can find common denominators by _____.

The product of two fractions is smaller than either of the factors because _____.

The quotient is not always smaller than the fractions being divided because _____.

</td>
</tr>
</table>

Difference from One Fraction Cards

$\dfrac{1}{2}$	$\dfrac{1}{3}$	$\dfrac{1}{4}$
$\dfrac{1}{5}$	$\dfrac{1}{6}$	$\dfrac{2}{3}$
$\dfrac{2}{4}$	$\dfrac{2}{5}$	$\dfrac{2}{6}$

Difference from One Fraction Cards *(cont.)*

$\dfrac{3}{4}$	$\dfrac{3}{5}$	$\dfrac{3}{6}$
$\dfrac{4}{5}$	$\dfrac{4}{6}$	$\dfrac{5}{6}$
$\dfrac{4}{4}$	$\dfrac{5}{5}$	$\dfrac{6}{6}$

Multiplication Chart

	1	2	3	4	5	6	7	8	9	10	11	12
1	1	2	3	4	5	6	7	8	9	10	11	12
2	2	4	6	8	10	12	14	16	18	20	22	24
3	3	6	9	12	15	18	21	24	27	30	33	36
4	4	8	12	16	20	24	28	32	36	40	44	48
5	5	10	15	20	25	30	35	40	45	50	55	60
6	6	12	18	24	30	36	42	48	54	60	66	72
7	7	14	21	28	35	42	49	56	63	70	77	84
8	8	16	24	32	40	48	56	64	72	80	88	96
9	9	18	27	36	45	54	63	72	81	90	99	108
10	10	20	30	40	50	60	70	80	90	100	110	120
11	11	22	33	44	55	66	77	88	99	110	121	132
12	12	24	36	48	60	72	84	96	108	120	132	144

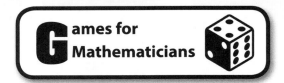

Games for Mathematicians

Dodge the Zombie

Overview

Students determine missing angle measurements to collect matching cards.

Materials

• *Dodge the Zombie Cards* (pages 29–31)

* The *Talking Points* card and these reproducibles are also provided in the Digital Resources (angle.pdf)

Objective

Use facts about supplementary, complementary, vertical, and adjacent angles to solve simple equations for an unknown angle in a figure.

Procedure

Note: Prior to the lesson, copy the *Dodge the Zombie Cards* (pages 29–31) on cardstock, cut, and laminate.

1. Distribute materials to students.

2. Players shuffle the cards and distribute them among players. Players do not need to have equal numbers of cards.

3. Players look at their hands and immediately set aside any cards that match. (A value of *x* is the missing angle measure.)

4. The first player offers his or her cards, facedown, to the player on his or her left, who takes one card from the offering.

5. If the card selected completes a match, the player sets aside the matching cards. The player then offers his or her cards, facedown, to the player on the left.

6. Play continues until only the zombie card is left. The player holding the zombie card loses the game.

7. Students may sketch and record their matching cards in their math journals.

Differentiation

• Provide visual supports for **below-level learners** who have difficulty remembering the relationships among angles.

• **Above-level learners** may create their own missing angle puzzles for an interactive bulletin board or workstation task.

Dodge the Zombie

Match missing angle measurements while avoiding the zombie!

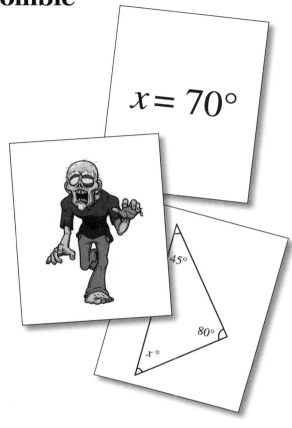

$x = 70°$

Materials

- *Dodge the Zombie Cards*

Directions

1. Shuffle the cards and distribute them among players. Players do not need to have equal numbers of cards.

2. Set aside any matching pairs of cards. (The value of x is the missing measurement.)

3. Player 1 offers his or her cards, facedown, to Player 2. Player 2 takes one card from Player 1.

4. If the card chosen completes a match, Player 2 sets aside the matching cards. Player 2 then offers his or her cards, facedown, to the next player.

5. Play continues until only the zombie card is left. Don't get caught holding the zombie card, or you lose!

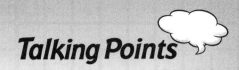

Talking Points

Talk like a mathematician:

Estimating a missing angle helps me _____.

Supplementary angles are different from complementary angles because _____.

Vertical angles are different from adjacent angles because_____.

I can find the missing angle in a triangle by _____.

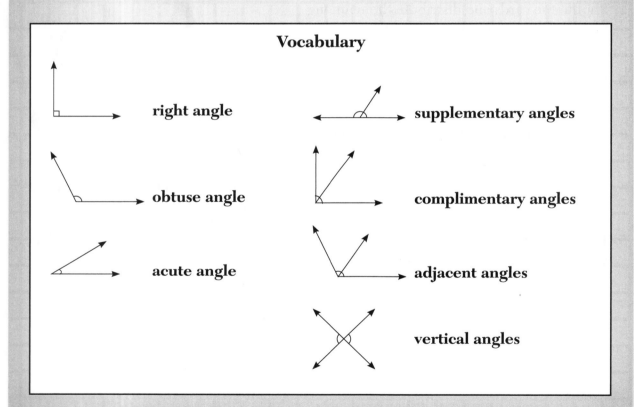

Vocabulary

right angle

obtuse angle

acute angle

supplementary angles

complimentary angles

adjacent angles

vertical angles

Dodge the Zombie Cards

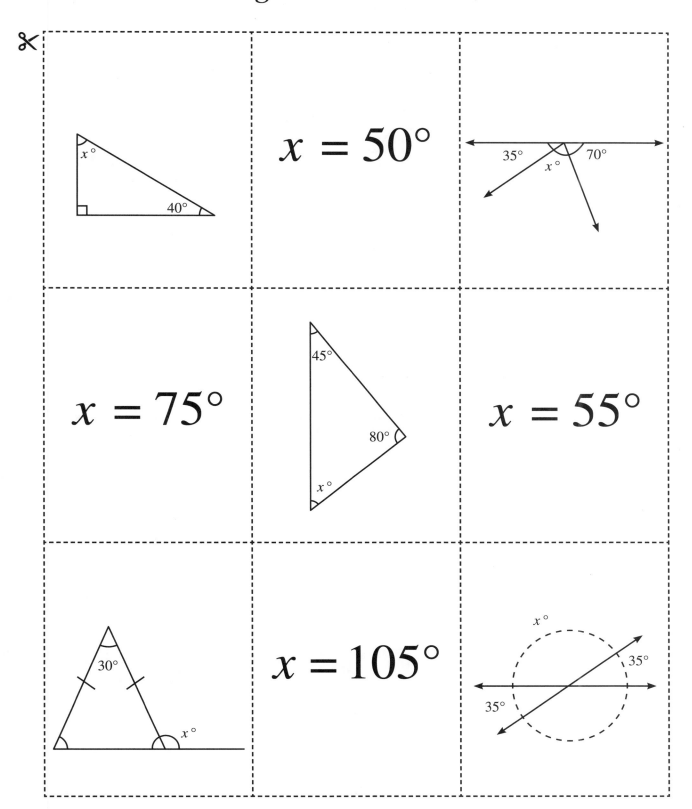

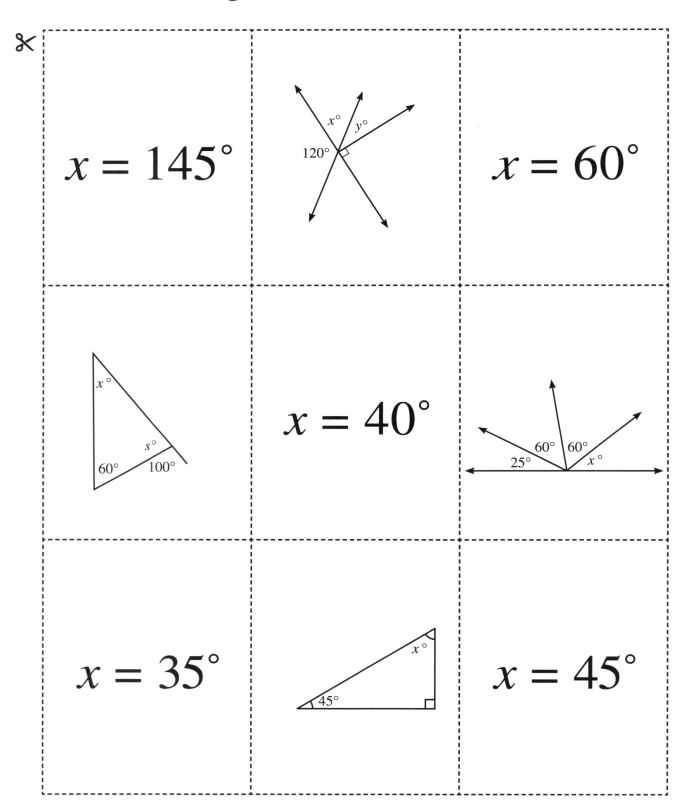

$x = 145°$

$x = 60°$

$x = 40°$

$x = 35°$

$x = 45°$

Dodge the Zombie Cards *(cont.)*

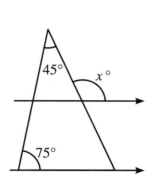

$$x = 120°$$

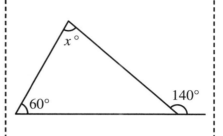

$$x = 80°$$

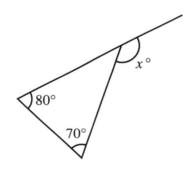

$$x = 150°$$

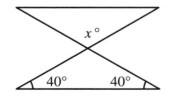

$$x = 100°$$

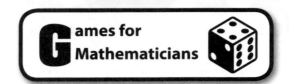

Games for **Mathematicians**

Integer Tug-of-War

- -

Overview

Players add and subtract positive and negative numbers to move the same playing piece back and forth, trying to be the first to reach their home space.

- -

Materials

- 1 game marker
- *Add/Subtract Spinner* (page 35)
- paper clip and pencil
- *Integer Tug-of-War Game Board* (page 36)
- standard playing cards (ace–9 only)

* The *Talking Points* card and these reproducibles are also provided in the Digital Resources (tugofwar.pdf)

Objective

Apply and extend previous understandings of numbers to the system of rational numbers by adding and subtracting integers.

Procedure

Note: Prior to introducing the workstation task, copy the *Add/Subtract Spinner* (page 35) and the *Integer-Tug-of-War Game Board* (page 36) on cardstock and laminate. Remove face cards from the deck of playing cards.

1. Distribute materials to students.

2. Players decide who will be Player 1 and Player 2 and place the game marker on the 0 space. Both players use the same playing piece.

3. Players shuffle the cards and place them facedown in a pile. Red suits (hearts and diamonds) represent negative numbers, and black suits (spades and clubs) represent positive numbers.

4. On each turn, players turn over the top card and move that many spaces toward their home space, spin the *Add/Subtract Spinner*, and create an equation using the number on the game board, the operation on the spinner, and the number on the card.

5. As the game progresses, the playing piece will move back and forth—similar to a game of tug-of-war. The first player to reach a homespace wins. Students may write their equations in their math journals.

Differentiation

- Have **below-level learners** play the game without the spinner to practice adding integers until they are ready to incorporate subtracting integers.

- Instruct **above-level learners** to spin the spinner twice and turn over two cards on each turn to add or subtract three integers.

Integer Tug-of-War

Add and subtract integers in a race to be the first player to reach the home space.

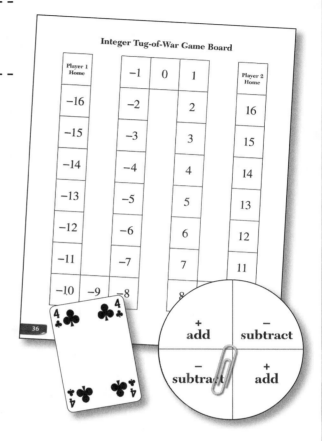

Materials

- 1 game marker
- *Add/Subtract Spinner*
- paper clip and pencil
- *Integer Tug-of-War Game Board*
- standard playing cards (ace–9 only)

Directions

1. Decide who will be Player 1 and Player 2.

2. Shuffle the cards and place them facedown.

3. Place the game marker on the space marked 0. (Both players use the same game marker.)

4. Take turns:

   - Turn over the top card and move that many spaces toward your home space.

   - Spin the spinner. Then, write an equation using the number on the game board, the operation on the spinner, and the number on the card. (Red cards represent negative numbers and black cards represent positive numbers.)

   - Solve the equation.

5. Be the first to reach your home space to win!

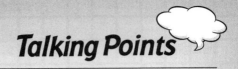

Talking Points

Vocabulary
• integer
• positive number
• negative number
• opposite

Talk like a mathematician:

Subtracting a negative number is like adding a positive number because _____.

The opposite of _____ is _____.

A number line is a useful model for adding and subtracting integers because _____.

A pattern I notice when adding integers is _____.

Talking Points

Vocabulary
• integer
• positive number
• negative number
• opposite

Talk like a mathematician:

Subtracting a negative number is like adding a positive number because _____.

The opposite of _____ is _____.

A number line is a useful model for adding and subtracting integers because _____.

A pattern I notice when adding positive and negative numbers is _____.

Add/Subtract Spinner

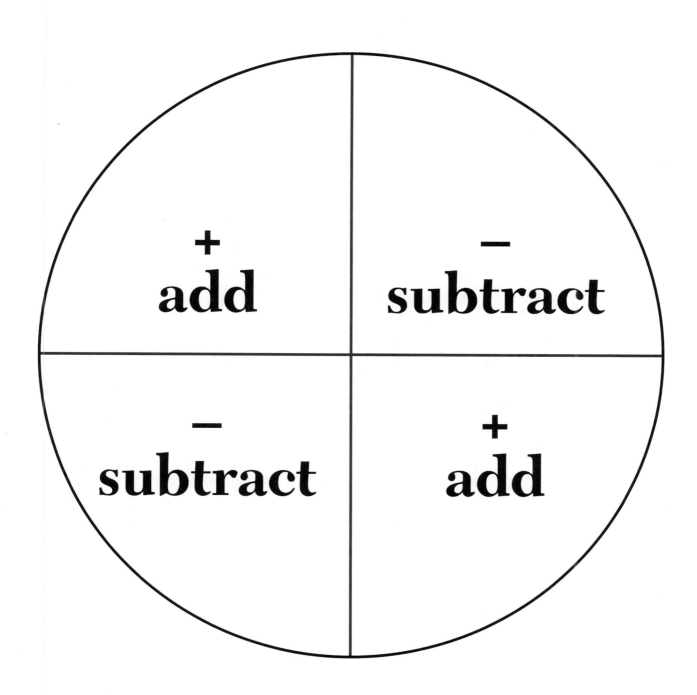

Integer Tug-of-War Game Board

Player 1 Home			−1	0	1		Player 2 Home
−16			−2		2		16
−15			−3		3		15
−14			−4		4		14
−13			−5		5		13
−12			−6		6		12
−11			−7		7		11
−10	−9	−8			8	9	10

51730—Guided Math Workstations

Exploring Manipulatives

- -

Overview

Students engage in unstructured exploration of manipulatives in preparation for organized use of during workstation tasks.

- -

Materials

- manipulatives (e.g., base-ten blocks, linking cubes, pattern blocks)

- digital device (optional)

- drawing or graph paper (optional)

* The *Talking Points* card and these reproducibles are also provided in the Digital Resources (manipulatives.pdf)

Objective

Make sense of problems and persevere in solving them.

Procedure

1. Place manipulatives in a workstation and allow students time to explore with them prior to using the manipulative for more formal math activities.

2. Provide drawing or graph paper for students who choose to create drawings of their manipulatives or record their thinking.

3. Consider having students use digital devices to take pictures of their explorations or record one another explaining their observations about the manipulatives.

Differentiation

Because of the nature of this activity, it is accessible to students of all ability levels, and students will naturally differentiate their explorations.

Exploring Manipulatives

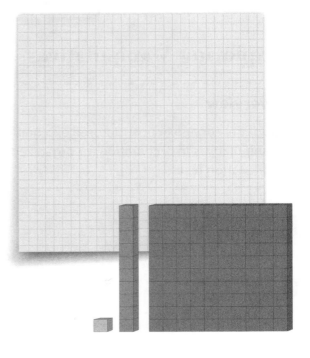

Explore math manipulatives and describe your observations.

Materials

- math manipulatives
- digital device, drawing paper, or graph paper

Directions

1. Take time to freely explore the math manipulative.

2. Think about how this manipulative might be a useful tool for mathematicians.

3. Record observations about the manipulative using words and pictures.

Talking Points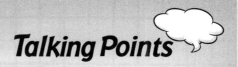

Vocabulary

- **manipulative**
- **attribute**
- **observe**
- **observations**
- **sort**

Talk like a mathematician:

An attribute of _____ is _____.

My observation is _____.

This manipulative is a useful tool because _____.

This manipulative reminds me of _____.

I can sort my manipulatives by _____.

✂ -

Talking Points

Vocabulary

- **manipulative**
- **attribute**
- **observe**
- **observations**
- **sort**

Talk like a mathematician:

An attribute of _____ is _____.

My observation is _____.

This manipulative is a useful tool because _____.

This manipulative reminds me of _____.

I can sort my manipulatives by _____.

Using What We Know

Cuisenaire® Rod Equations

- -

Overview

Students use Cuisenaire Rods® to create designs and write equations to describe the designs.

- -

Objective

Apply and extend previous understandings of arithmetic to algebraic expressions.

Procedure

Note: Allow time for students to freely explore with Cuisenaire® Rods before placing this task in a workstation.

1. Distribute copies of the *Centimeter Graph Paper* (page 43) and other materials to students.

2. Each student creates designs using the Cuisenaire® Rods. Then, students create a second design that has the same area as the first.

3. Students record their designs on the graph paper, label the pieces used, and write equations to describe the relationships between their figures.

4. Students check their equations by replacing the variables with their values.

5. You may collect students' graph paper showing their design sketches and equations.

Differentiation

- **Below-level learners** may create just one design and evaluate the expression.

- **Above-level learners** may explore ratios by assigning different values to the pieces. For example, if $w = 2$ (instead of 1), what is the value of the other pieces?

Cuisenaire® Rod Equations

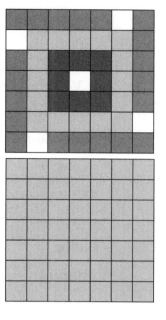

Create a design, and write a related equation.

Materials

- *Centimeter Graph Paper*
- Cuisenaire® Rods

Directions

1. Create a design using Cuisenaire® Rods.

2. Create a second design that has the same area as your first design.

3. Record your designs on the *Centimeter Graph Paper* and label the pieces you used.

4. Write an equation to describe the relationship between the two figures.

5. Check your equation by replacing the variables in your equations with their values and simplifying your equation.

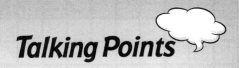

Talking Points

Vocabulary
• equation
• equivalent
• evaluate
• exponent
• expression
• factor
• product
• sum
• term
• variable

Talk like a mathematician:

To evaluate my expression, I _____.

A variable is _____.

My design shows _____.

My equation is true because _____.

A relationship I noticed is _____.

✂ ....

Talking Points

Vocabulary
• equation
• equivalent
• evaluate
• exponent
• expression
• factor
• product
• sum
• term
• variable

Talk like a mathematician:

To evaluate my expression, I _____.

A variable is _____.

My design shows _____.

My equation is true because _____.

A relationship I noticed is _____.

Centimeter Graph Paper

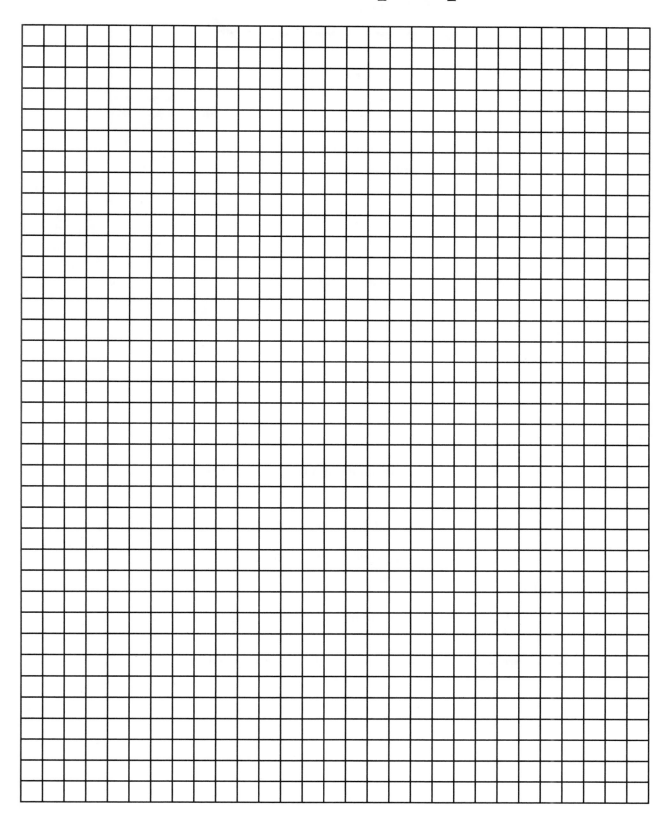

U sing What We Know

What's the Point?

Overview

Students use reasoning skills to justify the placement of missing decimal points in multiplication and division problems.

Materials

- *What's the Point? Cards* (pages 47–50)

- *Make Your Point* recording sheet (page 51)

* The *Talking Points* card and these reproducibles are also provided in the Digital Resources (point.pdf)

Objective

Make sense of quantities and their relationships and justify decisions using words, numbers, and pictures.

Procedure

Note: Prior to the lesson, copy the *What's the Point? Cards* (pages 47–50) on cardstock, cut, and laminate.

1. Distribute copies of the *Make Your Point* recording sheet (page 51) and other materials to students.

2. Students select cards in which the decimal point is missing in either the factors, the product, or the quotient.

3. Students determine where to place the decimal point(s) and justify their reasoning.

4. Students may show their thinking on their recording sheets.

Differentiation

- Simplify the problems for **below-level learners** who need additional support. Blank cards are provided.

- **Above-level learners** may create their own cards, which may then be added to the workstation for other students to use.

What's the Point?

Determine where to place missing decimal points in multiplication and division equations.

Materials

- *What's the Point? Cards*
- *Make Your Point* recording sheet

Directions

1. Select a *What's the Point? Card*. The calculations on these cards have already been done for you, but decimal points are missing.

2. Think like a mathematician to decide where the decimals points should go in the product, quotient, or factors.

3. Use precise mathematical language, numbers, and pictures to justify your decisions.

4. Record your thinking on the *Make Your Point* recording sheet.

Place the decimal in the product.

$6.25 \times 3.4 = 2125$

Place the decimal in the quotient.

$235.2 \div 98 = 24$

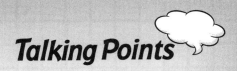

Vocabulary
- **estimate**
- **justify**

$$\begin{array}{r} 2.4 \\ \times\ \ 3 \\ \hline 7.2 \end{array}$$ factors

7.2 ← product
↑
decimal point

$$3\overline{)7.2}$$ 2.4 ← quotient
7.2 ← dividend
↑
divisor

Talk like a mathematician:

When finding the product of decimals, I notice that _____.

When deciding where to put the decimal point, I thought about _____.

My solution is reasonable because _____.

I can check my answer by _____.

Talking Points

Vocabulary
- **estimate**
- **justify**

$$\begin{array}{r} 2.4 \\ \times\ \ 3 \\ \hline 7.2 \end{array}$$ factors

7.2 ← product
↑
decimal point

$$3\overline{)7.2}$$ 2.4 ← quotient
7.2 ← dividend
↑
divisor

Talk like a mathematician:

When finding the product of decimals, I notice that _____.

When deciding where to put the decimal point, I thought about _____.

My solution is reasonable because _____.

I can check my answer by _____.

What's the Point? Cards

Place the decimal
in the product.

$6.25 \times 3.4 = 2125$

Place the decimal
in the product.

$0.45 \times 12.3 = 5535$

Place the decimal
in the product.

$11.68 \times 2.4 = 28032$

Place the decimal
in the product.

$3.01 \times 17.5 = 52675$

Place the decimal
in the product.

$0.37 \times 45.6 = 16872$

Place the decimal
in the product.

$22.3 \times 4.8 = 10704$

Place the decimal
in the product.

$5.04 \times 15.9 = 80136$

Place the decimal
in the product.

$60.2 \times 3.18 = 191436$

What's the Point? Cards *(cont.)*

Place the decimals in the factors. $303 \times 24 = 72.72$	Place the decimals in the factors. $56 \times 318 = 17.808$
Place the decimals in the factors. $18 \times 145 = 261.0$	Place the decimals in the factors. $65 \times 120 = 78.0$
Place the decimals in the factors. $58 \times 206 = 1194.8$	Place the decimals in the factors. $87 \times 248 = 21.576$
Place the decimals in the factors. $175 \times 602 = 105.35$	Place the decimals in the factors. $815 \times 204 = 1.6626$

What's the Point? Cards *(cont.)*

Place the decimal in the quotient. $76.5 \div 17 = 45$	Place the decimal in the quotient. $15.77 \div 38 = 415$
Place the decimal in the quotient. $235.2 \div 98 = 24$	Place the decimal in the quotient. $50.85 \div 4.5 = 113$
Place the decimal in the quotient. $6.656 \div 2.6 = 256$	Place the decimal in the quotient. $98.05 \div 5.3 = 185$
Place the decimal in the quotient. $9.168 \div 0.24 = 382$	Place the decimal in the quotient. $19.76 \div 6.5 = 304$

Place the decimal
in the product.

Place the decimal
in the product.

Place the decimal
in the product.

Place the decimals
in the factors.

Place the decimals
in the factors.

Place the decimals
in the factors.

Place the decimal
in the quotient.

Place the decimal
in the quotient.

Name: _____ Date: _____

Make Your Point

_____

_____

_____

_____

_____

_____

_____

Using What We Know

Graphing Growing Patterns

- -

Overview

Students use tiles to create patterns that grow both numerically and visually. Students display their patterns and represent them three different ways.

- -

Objective

Apply and extend previous understandings of arithmetic to algebraic expressions.

Procedure

Note: Students may work in pairs to facilitate mathematical conversations. A list of guiding questions is provided on the student task card to support discussion.

1. Distribute copies of the *Centimeter Graph Paper* (page 55) and other materials to students.

2. Once students are satisfied with their patterns, they may sketch and describe them on the graph paper or chart paper, or they may create digital presentations.

Differentiation

- To scaffold learning, provide **below-level learners** with simple patterns to duplicate and describe in multiple ways.

- Challenge **above-level learners** with a higher-level task by having them create and describe an original pattern.

- This task is self-differentiating because students will create more and less complicated patterns.

Graphing Growing Patterns

- -

Create a growing pattern, generalize the pattern, and describe it in multiple ways.

- -

Materials

- *Centimeter Graph Paper* or chart paper
- square tiles, pattern blocks, or cubes

Directions

1. Use square tiles, blocks, or cubes to create a growing pattern. Your pattern should grow both numerically and visually.

2. Consider these questions as you explore and create your pattern:

   - How does your pattern change numerically? Visually?
   - Could you create a different pattern that grows the same way numerically, but not visually?
   - How can you explain in words what is taking place in your pattern?
   - Can you create a generalized rule that will help you find the 100th term?
   - How many different ways can you explain your pattern?

3. Create a display. Include your pattern and at least three different ways to describe and represent it (e.g., describe in words, function table, graph, equation).

Talking Points

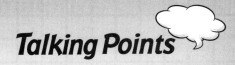

Vocabulary
• function
• generalize
• *y*-value
• *x*-value
• input
• output
• linear function
• non-linear function
• rate of change

Talk like a mathematician:

Representing functions in multiple ways helps to _____.

I can generalize my pattern by _____.

Functions can be used to solve problems by _____.

My pattern can/cannot be represented by a linear equation because _____.

Talking Points

Vocabulary
• function
• generalize
• *y*-value
• *x*-value
• input
• output
• linear function
• non-linear function
• rate of change

Talk like a mathematician:

Representing functions in multiple ways helps to _____.

I can generalize my pattern by _____.

Functions can be used to solve problems by _____.

My pattern can/cannot be represented by a linear equation because _____.

Centimeter Graph Paper

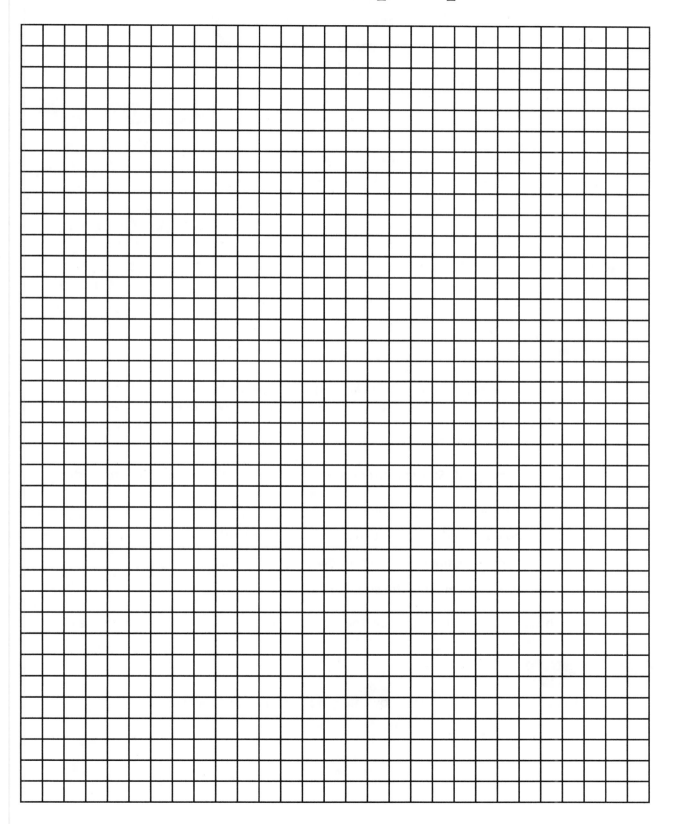

You Write the Story

Overview

Students are given equations with unknown numbers. They write story problems represented by the equations, draw mathematical models to show the problems, and solve the equations.

Materials

- *You Write the Story Cards* (pages 59–60)

- *My Story* recording sheet (page 61)

* Reproducibles for this task are provided in Digital Resources (story.pdf)

Objective

Represent and solve one- and two-step problems involving all four operations.

Procedure

Note: Prior to the lesson, copy the *You Write the Story Cards* (pages 59–60) on cardstock, cut, and laminate. A blank template is included to create cards for any type of equation: addition, subtraction, multiplication, division, computing with fractions or decimals, algebraic equations, and even multi-step problems.

1. Distribute copies of the *My Story* recording sheet (page 61) and other materials to students.

2. Students choose a card and do the following:

   • Write a story problem based on the equation shown on the card.

   • Draw a math picture or diagram to represent the story problem.

   • Solve for the unknown number in the equation.

3. You may choose to have students show their thinking in their math journals or on their recording sheets.

Differentiation

This activity may be easily differentiated by changing the equations that you use.

You Write the Story

Write a story problem to match an equation.

Materials

- *You Write the Story Cards*
- *My Story* recording sheet

Directions

1. Choose a *You Write the Story Card*.

2. Write a story problem to match the equation. (Make sure your story or diagram makes sense).

3. Draw a math picture or diagram to represent the story.

4. Solve for the unknown in the equation.

You Write the Story

$38.7 \div 3 = f$

You Write the Story

$100c = 26$

Talking Points

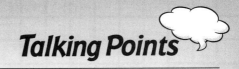

Vocabulary

- **sum**
- **difference**
- **addend**
- **equation**
- **diagram**
- **represent**

Talk like a mathematician:

I organized my thinking by _____.

The numbers in my story are reasonable because _____.

My picture represents my equation because _____.

I can check my solution by _____.

Another way to solve this problem is _____.

Talking Points

Vocabulary

- **sum**
- **difference**
- **addend**
- **equation**
- **diagram**
- **represent**

Talk like a mathematician:

I organized my thinking by _____.

The numbers in my story are reasonable because _____.

My picture represents my equation because _____.

I can check my solution by _____.

Another way to solve this problem is _____.

You Write the Story Cards

You Write the Story

$45m = \$393.75$

You Write the Story

$15 \div a = 30$

You Write the Story

$100c = 26$

You Write the Story

$38.7 \div 3 = f$

You Write the Story

$\dfrac{95}{5} - 3.6 = b$

You Write the Story

$(2.35 \times 6) + t = 21.1$

You Write the Story Cards *(cont.)*

You Write the Story

You Write the Story

You Write the Story

You Write the Story

You Write the Story

You Write the Story

Name: _____   Date: _____

My Story

Directions: Write a story problem that matches your equation. Draw a math picture or diagram that shows your story problem.

_____

_____

_____

_____

_____

_____

_____

Independent Math Work

Express Yourself

Materials

- *Express Yourself Cards* (pages 65–69)

- *Express Yourself Task Cards* (pages 70–71)

- *Express It* recording sheet (optional) (page 72)

* The *Talking Points* card and these reproducibles are also provided in the Digital Resources (express.pdf)

Overview

Students complete tasks relating algebraic expressions with written descriptions.

Objective

Use properties of operations to generate equivalent expressions.

Procedure

Note: Prior to the lesson, copy the *Express Yourself Cards* (pages 65–69) on cardstock, cut, and laminate.

1. Distribute copies of the *Express It* recording sheet (page 72) and other materials to students.

2. Assign *Express Yourself Task Cards* (pages 70–71) to students or allow them to choose. Each task card has a different set of instructions, including a bonus problem. Students may work individually, in pairs, or in groups.

3. Students complete the task from the *Express Yourself Task Card*. Students may show their thinking in their math journals or on their recording sheets.

Differentiation

- Support **below-level learners** with an anchor chart or reference sheet, showing the meanings of commonly used phrases (e.g., *increased* by means "addition").

- Challenge **above-level learners** to complete the bonus activities on the task card. You may also have students write additional matching cards to add to the workstation.

Express Yourself

Complete tasks relating algebraic
expressions with written descriptions.

Materials

- *Express Yourself Cards*
- *Express Yourself Task Cards*
- *Express It* recording sheet (optional)

Directions

1. Choose one of the *Express Yourself Task Cards*. Your teacher may specify which task you should complete.

2. Carefully read the directions for the task.

3. Complete the task and record your work either in your math journal or on the recording sheet.

Write It in Words

1. Choose five algebraic expressions cards.

2. Write the expressions using words two different ways in your math journal or on your *Express It* recording sheet.

Bonus: Write your own algebraic expression, and then write it using words two different ways.

Expression Sort

1. Choose 10 cards.

2. Sort the cards based on a common characteristic.

3. Show and explain how you sorted your cards using categories or a graphic organizer, such as a Venn diagram, in your math journal, or on your Express It recording sheet.

Bonus: Add several more expressions or phrases to your categories

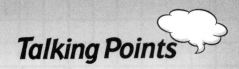

Vocabulary

- **algebraic expression**
- **equivalent expressions**
- **variable**
- **sum**
- **product**

Talk like a mathematician:

The algebraic expression means _____.

Thinking algebraically means _____.

I can use expressions to help me solve problems by _____.

The order in which I perform operations is important because _____.

Talking Points

Vocabulary

- **algebraic expression**
- **equivalent expressions**
- **variable**
- **sum**
- **product**

Talk like a mathematician:

The algebraic expression means _____.

Thinking algebraically means _____.

I can use expressions to help me solve problems by _____.

The order in which I perform operations is important because _____.

Express Yourself Cards

two more than some number	$x + 2$
two times a number increased by x	$2n + x$
some number plus 4 divided by 2	$\dfrac{x + 4}{2}$
the product of 2 and the sum of x and 4	$2(x + 4)$

Express Yourself Cards *(cont.)*

three times some number decreased by 4	$3t - 4$
the sum of four times t and 3	$4t + 3$
four less than the sum of three and t	$(3 + t) - 4$
take four away from t and divide the difference by 3	$\dfrac{t - 4}{3}$

Express Yourself Cards *(cont.)*

the sum of y and 8 divided by 3	$\dfrac{y + 8}{3}$
three divided by some number decreased by 8	$\dfrac{3}{y - 8}$
the product of eight and y increased by 3	$3 + 8y$
add three to the sum of 8 and y	$(8 + y) + 3$

ten less than some number	$y - 10$
ten increased by y	$10 + y$
the product of 10 and x added to some number	$10x + y$
ten reduced by some number times y	$y(10 - x)$

Express Yourself Cards *(cont.)*

5 divided by the sum of some number and 9	$$\dfrac{5}{w + 9}$$
nine more than the product of 5 and w	$$5w + 9$$
subtract five from 9 times some number	$$9w - 5$$
a number increased by five divided by 9	$$\dfrac{w + 5}{9}$$

Express Yourself Task Cards

Expression Match-Up

1. Arrange all of the cards faceup.

2. Find pairs of cards that show an algebraic expression and the matching description in words.

3. Record five of your matching pairs in your math journal or on the *Express It* recording sheet.

Bonus: For each of your matching pairs, write another way to describe the same expression in words.

Write It in Words

1. Choose five algebraic expressions cards.

2. Write the expressions using words two different ways in your math journal or on your *Express It* recording sheet.

Bonus: Write your own algebraic expression. Then, write it using words two different ways.

Express Yourself Task Cards (cont.)

Write an Expression

1. Choose 10 phrase cards.

2. Write algebraic expressions to match the phrases in your math journal or on your *Express It* recording sheet.

Bonus: Write a math story that could be solved using one of your algebraic expressions.

Expression Sort

1. Choose 10 cards.

2. Sort the cards based on a common characteristic.

3. Show and explain how you sorted your cards using categories or a graphic organizer, such as a Venn diagram, in your math journal, or on your *Express It* recording sheet.

Bonus: Add several more expressions or phrases to your categories.

Name: _____ Date: _____

Express It

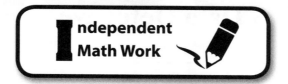

Independent Math Work

Data Detective

Overview

Students create dot plots from a set of data, calculate quantitative measures (mean, median, mode, and range), and make observations about the data.

Materials

- *Data Detective Cards* (pages 76–78)

- *Data Sleuth* recording sheet (page 79)

* The *Talking Points* card and these reproducibles are also provided in the Digital Resources (detective.pdf)

Objective

Display and summarize numerical data, give quantitative measures, and describe overall patterns.

Procedure

Note: Prior to the lesson, copy the *Data Detective Cards* (pages 76–78) on cardstock, cut, and laminate.

1. Distribute copies of the *Data Sleuth* recording sheet (page 79) and other materials to students.

2. Students choose a *Data Detective Card*.

3. Students create dot plots to display the data. These displays should include titles and labels.

4. Students calculate the mean, median, mode, and range, and connect these measures to real-life scenarios.

5. Students write three observations about their data.

6. You may choose to collect students' recording sheets or have students glue them in their math journals.

Differentiation

- For **below-level learners** who have difficulty working with larger sets of data, reduce the number of items in the data set and consider using numbers that are easier to work with.

- Challenge **above-level learners** to collect their own data for this task. Students may conduct a survey they create or use data from newspapers, magazines, or online research.

Data Detective

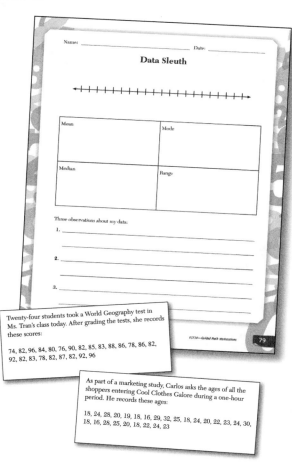

Create a dot plot from a set of data and describe the data using words and mathematical measures (mean, median, mode, and range).

Materials

- *Data Detective Cards*
- *Data Sleuth* recording sheet

Directions

1. Choose a *Data Detective Card*. Think about how a mathematician might organize the data to make it easier to work with.

2. Create a dot plot to show the data. Decide which numbers you will use to label your graph. Be sure to include a title and labels.

3. Calculate the mean, median, mode, and range of the data. Discuss how this is useful to you and the types of decisions it can help you make.

4. Write three observations about your data in your math journal or on your *Data Sleuth* recording sheet.

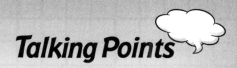
Vocabulary

- **data**
- **dot plot**
- **mean**
- **median**
- **mode**
- **range**
- **cluster**
- **gap**
- **outlier**

Talk like a mathematician:

I can organize my data by _____.

Another way to organize my data is _____.

I can find the median of my data by _____.

I can find the mode of my data by _____.

I can find the range of my data by _____.

I can find the mean of my data by _____.

The dot plot helps me to see that _____.

Talking Points

Vocabulary

- **data**
- **dot plot**
- **mean**
- **median**
- **mode**
- **range**
- **cluster**
- **gap**
- **outlier**

Talk like a mathematician:

I can organize my data by _____.

Another way to organize my data is _____.

I can find the median of my data by _____.

I can find the mode of my data by _____.

I can find the range of my data by _____.

I can find the mean of my data by _____.

The dot plot helps me to see that _____.

Data Detective Cards

Twenty-four students took a World Geography test in Ms. Tran's class today. After grading the tests, she records these scores:

74, 82, 96, 84, 80, 76, 90, 82, 85, 83, 88, 86, 78, 86, 82, 92, 82, 83, 78, 82, 87, 82, 92, 96

As part of a marketing study, Carlos asks the ages of all the shoppers entering Cool Clothes Galore during a one-hour period. He records these ages:

18, 24, 28, 20, 19, 18, 16, 29, 32, 25, 18, 24, 20, 22, 23, 24, 30, 18, 16, 28, 25, 20, 18, 22, 24, 23

Mr. Carlson's students are conducting an experiment to study the effect of fertilizer on the growth of bean plants. They record the heights, in inches, of the bean plants they are growing:

8, 12, 10, 16, 22, 10, 24, 15, 20, 9, 28, 16, 10, 11, 10, 22, 24, 27, 14, 12, 16, 26, 22, 20, 22, 8

Data Detective Cards *(cont.)*

Everton's basketball team played twenty games this season. This list shows the points they scored in each game:

48, 42, 38, 52, 39, 38, 54, 40, 52, 36, 50, 38, 50, 42, 44, 37, 40, 38, 41, 51

A police officer monitors the speed of cars passing through a school zone. The speed limit in the school zone is 25 miles per hour. The officer records these speeds:

24, 25, 25, 23, 26, 30, 21, 25, 25, 24, 28, 28, 22, 25, 24, 26, 27, 32, 24, 25, 28, 25, 25, 24, 26, 28, 24

The student council collects used books to donate to a homeless shelter. The books collected by each class are shown in this list:

4, 28, 20, 14, 20, 19, 24, 26, 20, 28, 8, 12, 15, 20, 22, 27, 9, 18, 12, 24, 29, 21, 25, 20, 12

Brandon took part in a bass fishing tournament. This list shows the weight, in pounds, of the top 20 largemouth bass that were caught during the tournament:

12, 8, 14, 15, 9, 8, 13, 12, 10, 16, 7, 9, 12, 11, 14, 11, 10, 8, 13, 12

Lucas surveyed his classmates to find out how long they take to get ready for school each morning. This list shows the minutes spent by each student:

21, 32, 28, 40, 25, 20, 45, 42, 38, 29, 30, 24, 45, 40, 23, 28, 35, 38, 42, 35, 25, 25, 30, 45, 24

A coach took the resting heart rate in beats per minute of each player on a baseball team before they began practice. This list show the players' heart rates:

65, 68, 58, 70, 78, 65, 80, 54, 72, 68, 75, 60, 62, 78, 58, 60, 75, 62, 60, 76, 70, 68, 59, 70, 61

Name: _____ Date: _____

Data Sleuth

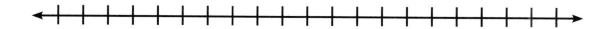

Mean	Mode
Median	Range

Three observations about my data

1. _____

   _____

2. _____

   _____

3. _____

   _____

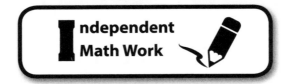

Slope and Intercept

- -

Overview

Students choose cards with a *y*-intercept and one ordered pair, and graph the line. Then, students find the slopes of the lines and write equations in slope-intercept form.

- -

Materials

- *Y-Intercept Cards* (page 83)

- *Ordered Pair Cards* (page 84)

- *Graph the Line* recording sheet (page 85)

* The *Talking Points* card and these reproducibles are also provided in the Digital Resources (slope.pdf)

Objective

Graph a line, determine the slope of the line, and derive the slope-intercept form.

Procedure

Note: Prior to the lesson, copy *Y-Intercept* and *Ordered Pairs Card* (pages 83–84) on cardstock, cut, and laminate.

1. Distribute copies of the *Graph the Line* recording sheet (page 85) and other materials to students.

2. Students choose a Y-*Intercept* card and an *Ordered Pair* card.

3. Students plot the *y*-intercept and the ordered pair. Then, graph the line using one of the coordinate grids on the recording sheet.

4. Students determine the slope of the line (rise over run).

5. Students use the *y*-intercept and slope to describe their lines using slope-intercept form.

6. You may choose to collect students' recording sheet.

Differentiation

- Have **below-level learners** review and practice linear equation concepts online using guided instructional videos.

- Instruct **above-level learners** to choose two ordered pair cards, graph the line, and find both the slope and *y*-intercept.

Slope and Intercept

Graph a line using the y-intercept and one ordered pair. Then, find the slope of the line and write the slope-intercept form for the line.

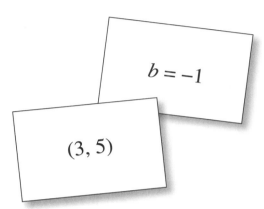

Materials

- *Y-Intercept Cards*
- *Ordered Pair Cards*
- *Graph the Line* recording sheet

$$\text{Slope} = \frac{\text{rise}}{\text{run}} = \frac{\Delta y}{\Delta x} = \frac{y_2 - y_1}{x_2 - x_1}$$

Slope-intercept form: $y = mx + b$
m is the slope of the line
b is the y-intercept
The y-intercept is the point where the line crosses the y-axis.

Directions

1. Choose a *Y-Intercept Card* and an *Ordered Pair Card*.

2. On your *Graph the Line* recording sheet, plot the y-intercept and the ordered pair. Then, graph the line.

3. Determine the slope of the line. Justify your answer using the formula for finding slope.

4. Describe the line using slope-intercept form.

Challenge

Choose two *Ordered Pair Cards*, graph the line, find both the slope and y-intercept, and describe the line in slope-intercept form.

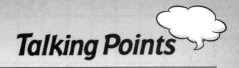

Vocabulary
• **linear equation**
• **x-axis**
• **y-axis**
• **ordered pair**
• **y-intercept**
• **slope**
• **slope-intercept form**
• **rise**
• **run**

Talk like a mathematician:

A pattern I notice on my graph is _____.

Modeling on a graph helps me _____.

The relationship between the graph and the line is _____.

If the slope is negative, I know _____.

A positive slope tells me _____.

Talking Points

Vocabulary
• **linear equation**
• **x-axis**
• **y-axis**
• **ordered pair**
• **y-intercept**
• **slope**
• **slope-intercept form**
• **rise**
• **run**

Talk like a mathematician:

A pattern I notice on my graph is _____.

Modeling on a graph helps me _____.

The relationship between the graph and the line is _____.

If the slope is negative, I know _____.

A positive slope tells me _____.

Y-Intercept Cards

$b = -1$	$b = -2$	$b = -3$
$b = -4$	$b = -5$	$b = -6$
$b = 0$	$b = 0$	$b = 0$
$b = 1$	$b = 2$	$b = 3$
$b = 4$	$b = 5$	$b = 6$

Ordered Pairs Cards

(−2, 3)	(4, 2)	(3, 5)
(1, 6)	(−3, −4)	(−6, 2)
(3, 1)	(−4, 1)	(−5, −2)
(2, 3)	(6, −3)	(−1, 5)
(−3, 3)	(1, 4)	(4, −5)

Name: _____ Date: _____

Graph the Line

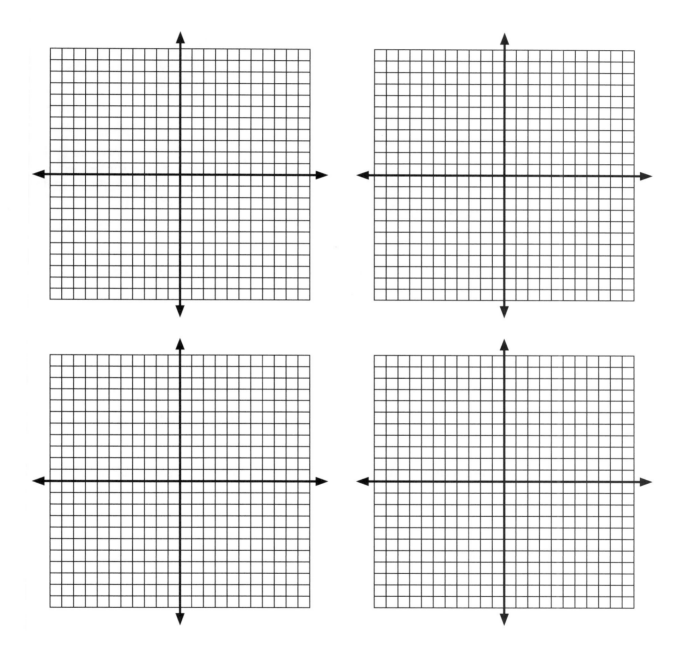

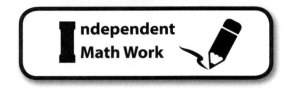

Independent Math Work

Rate and Ratio Task Cards

Overview

Students represent and solve real-life rate and ratio problems using a rate table, bar model, or double number line.

Materials

- *Rate and Ratio Task Cards* (pages 89–92)

- *Representation* recording sheet (page 93)

* The *Talking Points* card and these reproducibles are also provided in the Digital Resources (rate.pdf)

Objective

Solve real-world problems using ratio and rate reasoning.

Procedure

Note: Prior to introducing the workstation, copy and cut apart the *Rate and Ratio Task Cards* (pages 89–92).

1. You may choose to select one problem for all students to complete or provide several for students to select from.

2. Distribute copies of the *Representation* recording sheet (page 93) to students. Each student will glue their problem on their recording sheet.

3. Students will choose representations that help solve the problem: rate table, bar model, or a double number line.

4. Students should phrase solutions as complete sentences as a check of reasonableness.

Differentiation

- Provide partially constructed rate tables to support **below-level learners**.

- Challenge **above-level learners** to construct graphs showing their rates and ratios.

Rate and Ratio Task Cards

Represent and solve real-world problems using a rate table, bar model, or double number line.

> The ratio of sugar to flour in a brownie recipe is 8:5. Laura used 15 ounces of flour.
>
> How many ounces of sugar did Laura use?

Materials

- *Rate and Ratio Task Cards*
- *Representation* recording sheet

> A contractor used 4 sheets of plywood and 112 nails to construct one wall in a house. He estimates he will use 18 sheets of plywood for the walls in two rooms.
>
> How many nails will he need?

Directions

1. Glue your problem on your *Representation* recording sheet.

2. Read your problem carefully to make sure you understand the story.

3. Decide which representation you want to use to solve the problem: a rate table, bar model, or double number line. You might need to try more than one representation to find the best option.

4. Create your representation. Be sure to use labels and numbers to communicate your mathematical thinking.

5. Write your solution as a complete sentence. Be sure your solution is reasonable.

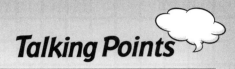

Talking Points

Vocabulary
• ratio
• rate
• unit rate
• ratio table

Talk like a mathematician:

I chose to represent this problem using a _____ because _____.

A pattern I notice is _____.

Using a _____ to solve the problem helped me by _____.

My solution makes sense because _____.

Talking Points

Vocabulary
• ratio
• rate
• unit rate
• ratio table

Talk like a mathematician:

I chose to represent this problem using a _____ because _____.

A pattern I notice is _____.

Using a _____ to solve the problem helped me by _____.

My solution makes sense because _____.

Rate and Ratio Task Cards

The ratio of sugar to flour in a brownie recipe is 8:5. Kimo used 15 ounces of flour.

How many ounces of sugar did Kimo use?

A contractor used 4 sheets of plywood and 112 nails to construct one wall in a house. She estimates she will use 18 sheets of plywood for the walls in two rooms.

How many nails will she need?

A candy store sells licorice mix for $6.08 per pound.

How much would it cost to buy $3\frac{1}{2}$ pounds of licorice mix?

Rate and Ratio Task Cards *(cont.)*

Yummy Bakery sold 108 doughnuts on Friday morning. The ratio of cups of coffee sold to doughnuts sold was 4:9.

How many cups of coffee did Yummy Bakery sell?

The Museum of Natural Science has a large collection of spiders and insects. The collection includes 420 spiders. The ratio of spiders to insects is 15:12.

How many total insects and spiders are in the collection?

A pet store sells 3 beta fish for $29.85. On Friday, they sold 17 beta fish.

How much money did they make selling beta fish on Friday?

Rate and Ratio Task Cards *(cont.)*

A small business owner ships jars of homemade honey. Four jars weigh a total of 7.4 pounds.

How much will 24 jars weigh?

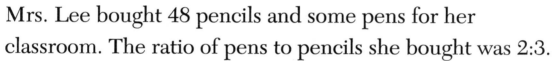

Mrs. Lee bought 48 pencils and some pens for her classroom. The ratio of pens to pencils she bought was 2:3.

How many pens did Mrs. Lee buy?

Sid and Jennifer were training for a race. For every mile that Sid ran, Jennifer ran $1\frac{3}{4}$ miles. Sid ran 5 miles this week.

How many miles did Jennifer run this week?

Rate and Ratio Task Cards *(cont.)*

LaShawn is taking a trip. He will drive 455 miles, and he gets an average of 17.5 miles per gallon in his truck. Gas costs an average of $3.25 per gallon.

How much money should LaShawn budget for the gas on his trip?

The ratio of windows to floors in an office building is 18:2. There are 126 windows in the building.

How many floors does the office building contain?

Eduardo uses the same number of beads on each bracelet he makes for his friends. He used 45 beads to make 3 bracelets.

How many bracelets can Eduardo make with 135 beads?

Name: _____   Date: _____

Representation

(glue task card here)

Write your solution as a complete sentence: _____

_____

_____

Developing **Fluency**

Greatest Common Factor Bingo

Overview

Students determine the greatest common factor of two numbers and claim the corresponding space on a bingo game board. An alternate game connects greatest common factors to the distributive property.

Objectives

- Find the greatest common factor (GCF) of two numbers less than or equal to 100.

- Use the distributive property to express a sum of two whole numbers 1–100 with a common factor as a multiple of a sum of two whole numbers with no common factor.

Procedure

Note: Prior to the lesson, copy the *GCF Bingo Cards* (pages 97–100) on cardstock, cut, and laminate. Determine whether students will play Game 1 (page 101) or Game 2 (page 102).

1. Distribute materials to students.

2. Players fill in the spaces on their *GCF Bingo Game Boards*. Students mark the spaces at random using numbers (Game 1) or expressions (Game 2) from the top of the board.

3. Students shuffle the cards and place them facedown in a pile.

4. Players turn over the top card. Students either find the greatest common factor of the two numbers listed on the card (Game 1), or evaluate the expression shown on the card (Game 2). They should show their calculations in their math journals or their *GCF* recording sheets. Students mark the space on their game boards that shows the GCF of two numbers (Game 1) or the value of the expression as the sum of two whole numbers (Game 2).

5. The first player to get four in a row wins.

Differentiation

- Provide **below-level learners** with *Multiplication/Division Charts* (page 104) and *Addition/ Subtraction Charts* (page 105). Include visuals that show several strategies for finding the greatest common factor of two numbers.

- **Above-level learners** may write word problems involving real-life applications of greatest common factors.

Materials

- *GCF Bingo Cards* (Game 1) (pages 97–98)

- *GCF Bingo Cards* (Game 2) (pages 99–100)

- *GCF Bingo Game Board* (Game 1) (page 101)

- *GCF Bingo Game Board* (Game 2) (page 102)

- dry erase markers

- *GCF* recording sheet (optional) (page 103)

- *Multiplication/Division Chart* (optional) (page 104)

- *Addition/Subtraction Chart* (optional) (page 105)

* The *Talking Points* card and these reproducibles are also provided in the Digital Resources (bingo.pdf)

Greatest Common Factor Bingo

Game 1: Determine the greatest common factor (GCF) of two numbers and claim the corresponding space on a bingo game board.

Game 2: Match the sum of two whole numbers with an expression that uses the distributive property to show the sum another way.

Materials

- *GCF Bingo Cards*
- *GCF Bingo Game Board*
- dry erase markers
- *GCF recording sheet* (optional)

Directions

1. Write FREE in any space on your game board.

   - Game 1: Mark the spaces at random using the numbers at the top of the board.
   - Game 2: Mark the spaces at random using the expressions at the top of the board.

2. Shuffle the cards and place them facedown in a pile. Turn over the top card.

   - Game 1: Find the GCF of the two numbers listed on the card. Show your calculations in your math journal or *GCF recording sheet*. Mark the space on your game board showing the GCF of the two numbers.
   - Game 2: Evaluate the expression shown on the card. Show your calculations in your math journal or *GCF recording sheet*. Mark the space on your game board that shows the value of the expression as the sum of two whole numbers.

3. Continue turning over cards and marking spaces.

4. Mark four spaces in a row first to win!

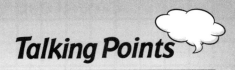

Talking Points

Vocabulary

- factor
- greatest common factor
- multiple
- product
- sum
- addend
- distributive property
- prime number
- composite number
- prime factorization

Talk like a mathematician:

The greatest common factor of _____ and _____ is _____.

A pattern I notice when finding a greatest common factor is _____.

One way to find the greatest common factor is _____.

Another way to find the greatest common factor is _____.

Talking Points

Vocabulary

- factor
- greatest common factor
- multiple
- product
- sum
- addend
- distributive property
- prime number
- composite number
- prime factorization

Talk like a mathematician:

The greatest common factor of _____ and _____ is _____.

A pattern I notice when finding a greatest common factor is _____.

One way to find the greatest common factor is _____.

Another way to find the greatest common factor is _____.

GCF Bingo Cards (Game 1)

What is the GCF of 27 and 6?

What is the GCF of 56 and 24?

What is the GCF of 32 and 12?

What is the GCF of 10 and 35?

What is the GCF of 42 and 28?

What is the GCF of 35 and 14?

What is the GCF of 30 and 36?

What is the GCF of 22 and 50?

GCF Bingo Cards (Game 1) *(cont.)*

What is the GCF of 72 and 63?	What is the GCF of 18 and 48?
What is the GCF of 39 and 12?	What is the GCF of 28 and 60?
What is the GCF of 57 and 21?	What is the GCF of 16 and 39?
What is the GCF of 36 and 84?	

GCF Bingo Cards (Game 2)

$3(9 + 2)$	$8(7 + 3)$
$4(8 + 3)$	$5(2 + 7)$
$14(3 + 2)$	$7(5 + 2)$
$6(5 + 6)$	$2(11 + 25)$

9(8 + 7)	6(3 + 8)
3(13 + 4)	4(7 + 15)
3(19 + 7)	12(3 + 7)
1(16 + 39)	

GCF Bingo Game Board (Game 1)

Directions: Write FREE in any space. Randomly write the following numbers in the remaining spaces: 1, 2, 3, 3, 3, 4, 4, 5, 6, 6, 7, 8, 9, 12, 14.

GCF Bingo Game Board (Game 2)

Directions: Write FREE in any space. Randomly write the following expressions in the remaining spaces:

27 + 6	10 + 35	30 + 36	18 + 48	57 + 21
56 + 24	42 + 28	22 + 50	39 + 12	36 + 84
32 + 12	35 + 14	72 + 63	28 + 60	16 + 39

51730—*Guided Math Workstations*

Name: _____ Date: _____

GCF

_____

_____

_____

_____

_____

_____

_____

Multiplication/Division Chart

×/÷	1	2	3	4	5	6	7	8	9
1	1	2	3	4	5	6	7	8	9
2	2	4	6	8	10	12	14	16	18
3	3	6	9	12	15	18	21	24	27
4	4	8	12	16	20	24	28	32	36
5	5	10	15	20	25	30	35	40	45
6	6	12	18	24	30	36	42	48	54
7	7	14	21	28	35	42	49	56	63
8	8	16	24	32	40	48	56	64	72
9	9	18	27	36	45	54	63	72	81

Addition/Subtraction Chart

+/−	1	2	3	4	5	6	7	8	9	10
1	2	3	4	5	6	7	8	9	10	11
2	3	4	5	6	7	8	9	10	11	12
3	4	5	6	7	8	9	10	11	12	13
4	5	6	7	8	9	10	11	12	13	14
5	6	7	8	9	10	11	12	13	14	15
6	7	8	9	10	11	12	13	14	15	16
7	8	9	10	11	12	13	14	15	16	17
8	9	10	11	12	13	14	15	16	17	18
9	10	11	12	13	14	15	16	17	18	19
10	11	12	13	14	15	16	17	18	19	20

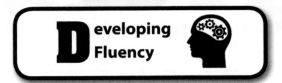

Developing Fluency

Integer Battle

Overview

Students win cards by adding a series of positive and negative numbers and having the greatest sum.

Objectives

- Understand that positive and negative numbers describe quantities having opposite values.
- Add and subtract positive and negative numbers.

Materials

- standard deck of playing cards
- number cube
- *Integer Battle* recording sheet (page 109)
- *Number Line* (optional) (page 110)
- * The *Talking Points* card and these reproducibles are also provided in the Digital Resources (battle.pdf)

Procedure

Note: Prior to the lesson, remove the face cards (jack, queen, and king) from the deck. Aces count as 1.

1. Distribute copies of the *Integer Battle* recording sheet (page 109) and other materials to students.

2. Students deal the cards. It is not important for each player to have exactly the same number of cards.

3. For each hand, one player rolls a number cube. The number rolled is the number of cards each player turns over. Cards with a black suit (spaces and clubs) are positive numbers, while cards with a red suit (hearts and diamonds) are negative numbers.

4. Players write their expressions either in their math journals or on their recording sheets and evaluate the expression, showing the strategy they used. For example, players might combine numbers with like signs or combine like numbers with opposite signs.

5. The player with the greatest sum takes all the cards. If players have equal sums, the cards go to the winner of the next round.

6. Students may show their calculations in their math journals or on their recording sheets.

Differentiation

- Have **below-level learners** turn over only two cards each round, rather than rolling the number cube. You may also provide the *Number Line* (page 110) as a visual support.

- **Above-level learners** may use operation cards with addition, subtraction, and multiplication. Players turn over three number cards and two operation cards and combine the cards in any order to create the greatest result.

Integer Battle

Win cards by adding positive and negative numbers and having the greatest sum.

Materials

- standard deck of playing cards
- number cube
- *Integer Battle* recording sheet

Directions

1. Shuffle and deal the cards. It is not important that players have exactly the same number of cards.

2. Take turns:

   - Roll the number cube. The number rolled is the number of cards each player turns over. Cards with black suits (spades and clubs) represent positive numbers, and cards with red suits (hearts and diamonds) represent negative numbers.
   - Record and evaluate your numerical expression in your math journal or *Integer Battle* recording sheet. Be sure to show your strategy and mathematical thinking.

3. If you have the greatest value, take all the cards. If sums are equal, the winner of the next round takes the cards.

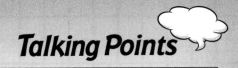

Talking Points

Vocabulary
• numerical expressions
• evaluate
• sum
• positive
• negative
• opposite numbers
• greatest
• least

Talk like a mathematician:

The strategy I used to evaluate my expression is _____.

_____ is greater than _____ because _____.

_____ is the opposite of _____.

To add a negative number, I can _____.

Talking Points

Vocabulary
• numerical expressions
• evaluate
• sum
• positive
• negative
• opposite numbers
• greatest
• least

Talk like a mathematician:

The strategy I used to evaluate my expression is _____.

_____ is greater than _____ because _____.

_____ is the opposite of _____.

To add a negative number, I can _____.

Name: _____ Date: _____

Integer Battle

Number Line

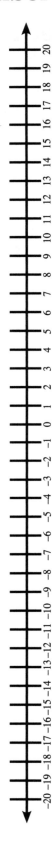

Developing **Fluency**

Scientific Notation

Overview

Students convert numbers written in scientific notation to standard form and perform operations with numbers expressed in scientific notation.

Objectives

- Use numbers expressed in the form of a single digit multiplied by an integer power of 10 to estimate very large or very small quantities

- Perform operations with numbers expressed in scientific notation.

Materials

- *Scientific Notation Task Cards* (pages 114–119)

- *Number Conversion* recording sheet (page 120)

- *Scientific Notation Operations* recording sheet (optional) (page 121)

* The *Talking Points* card and these reproducibles are also provided in the Digital Resources (scientific.pdf)

Procedure

Note: Prior to introducing the workstation task, copy the *Scientific Notation Task Cards* (pages 114–119) on cardstock, cut, and laminate.

1. Distribute copies of the *Number Conversion* recording sheet (page 120) and other materials to students.

2. Some or all task cards may be used at one time. For example, you might only use the cards for converting from scientific notation to standard form or only the cards for converting from standard form to scientific notation before using all the task cards.

3. Students choose up to 10 cards and record both the standard form and scientific notation on the *Number Conversion* recording sheet.

4. An optional *Scientific Notation Operations* recording sheet (page 121) is included to provide practice performing operations with numbers expressed in scientific notation.

5. You may choose to collect students' recording sheets.

Differentiation

- Scaffold learning for **below-level learners** by preparing cards with less complex numbers, building up to the numbers provided in this task. For example, use numbers such as 5×10^3 or 0.075.

- Challenge **above-level learners** to find real-world examples of very small or very large numbers and express the numbers in scientific notation.

Scientific Notation

Task 1: Convert between scientific notation and standard form to express very small and very large numbers.

Task 2: Perform operations with numbers expressed in scientific notation.

Materials

- *Scientific Notation Task Cards*
- *Number Conversion* recording sheet
- *Scientific Notation Operations* recording sheet

Directions

Task 1:

1. Choose one *Scientific Notation Task Card*.

2. Follow the directions on the card and record your calculations on the *Number Conversion* recording sheet.

Task 2:

1. Choose six *Scientific Notation Task Cards*.

2. Use the six cards to create one addition problem, one multiplication problem, and one subtraction problem.

3. Show your solutions on the *Scientific Notation Operations* recording sheet.

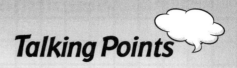

Talking Points

Vocabulary

- **exponent**
- **base number**
- **power**
- **scientific notation**
- **standard form**

Talk like a mathematician:

Scientific notation is helpful when working with very small or very large numbers because _____.

I can convert a number from standard form to scientific notation by _____.

I can change a number written in standard form to scientific notation by _____.

A negative exponent means that _____.

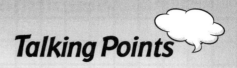

Talking Points

Vocabulary

- **exponent**
- **base number**
- **power**
- **scientific notation**
- **standard form**

Talk like a mathematician:

Scientific notation is helpful when working with very small or very large numbers because _____.

I can convert a number from standard form to scientific notation by _____.

I can change a number written in standard form to scientific notation by _____.

A negative exponent means that _____.

Scientific Notation Task Cards

Write the number

2,300,000,000

in scientific notation.

Write the number

37,000,000

in scientific notation.

Write the number

68,500,000

in scientific notation.

Write the number

48,000,000,000

in scientific notation.

Write the number

500,000

in scientific notation.

Write the number

705,000,000

in scientific notation.

Write the number

90,000,000

in scientific notation.

Write the number

350,000,000

in scientific notation.

Scientific Notation Task Cards *(cont.)*

Write the number

0.000000345

in scientific notation.

Write the number

0.000024

in scientific notation.

Write the number

0.0000701

in scientific notation.

Write the number

0.0006

in scientific notation.

Write the number

0.00000067

in scientific notation.

Write the number

0.0000005

in scientific notation.

Write the number

0.000000314

in scientific notation.

Write the number

0.0000098

in scientific notation.

Scientific Notation Task Cards *(cont.)*

Express 3.8×10^8 in standard form.	Express 2.06×10^3 in standard form.
Express 9×10^6 in standard form.	Express 6.5×10^5 in standard form.
Express 8.55×10^4 in standard form.	Express 1.4×10^7 in standard form.
Express 1.25×10^5 in standard form.	Express 7.3×10^6 in standard form.

51730—Guided Math Workstations

Scientific Notation Task Cards *(cont.)*

Express
5.8×10^{-5}
in standard form.

Express
6.22×10^{-4}
in standard form.

Express
2.03×10^{-6}
in standard form.

Express
7×10^{-3}
in standard form.

Express
9.1×10^{-7}
in standard form.

Express
1.75×10^{-6}
in standard form.

Express
8×10^{-9}
in standard form.

Express
4.6×10^{-7}
in standard form.

Write the number in scientific notation.	Write the number in scientific notation.
Write the number in scientific notation.	Write the number in scientific notation.
Write the number in scientific notation.	Write the number in scientific notation.
Write the number in scientific notation.	Write the number in scientific notation.

Scientific Notation Task Cards *(cont.)*

Express	Express
in standard form.	in standard form.
Express	Express
in standard form.	in standard form.
Express	Express
in standard form.	in standard form.
Express	Express
in standard form.	in standard form.

Name: _____ Date: _____

Number Conversion

Directions: Record the scientific notation and standard form for each card you draw.

Scientific Notation	Standard Form

Scientific Notation Operations

Directions: Choose six cards. Use all six cards to complete the tasks below.

Find the sum of two of your cards.

Find the difference of two of your remaining cards.

Find the product your last two cards.

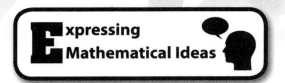
Expressing Mathematical Ideas

Making Connections

- -

Overview

Students roll two number cubes to choose a vocabulary word and describe personal connections, mathematical connections, and real-world connections to the word.

- -

Objective

Make sense of mathematics by formulating personal, mathematical, and real-world connections to mathematical concepts.

Procedure

Materials

- 2 number cubes
- *Vocabulary Board* (page 125)
- *Making Connections* graphic organizer (page 126)
- *Compare and Contrast* graphic organizer (optional) (page 127)
- * The *Talking Points* card and these reproducibles are also provided in the Digital Resources (connections.pdf)

1. Distribute copies of the *Making Connections* graphic organizer (page 126) and other materials to students.

2. Students roll two number cubes and find the space where the two numbers intersect on their *Vocabulary Board* (page 125). This gives each student a choice of two words. For example, a roll of 1 and 3 could be used as column 1 and row 3 or column 3 and row 1.

3. Using the word, students complete the *Making Connections* graphic organizer to describe connections to the vocabulary word.

   - **My connections**—Students describe personal connections to the vocabulary term. A student's connections to *percent*, for example, might be the grade they earned on a quiz.

   - **Math connections**—Students describe connections to other mathematical concepts. A mathematical connection for *percent* might be a connection to fractions or decimals.

   - **Real-world connections**—Students describe ways in which they might see this mathematical concept in everyday life. An example would be the connection between *percent* and the savings during a sale at a clothing store.

4. You may choose to collect students' graphic organizers.

Differentiation

- Support **below-level learners** by creating graphic organizers with some of the connections completed. Provide them with a word bank (or use the *Vocabulary Board*), and have them complete the *Making Connections* graphic organizer.

- Have **above-level learners** use both words from the roll, complete the *Making Connections* graphic organizer for both, and compare and contrast the two words using the *Compare and Contrast* graphic organizer (page 127).

Making Connections

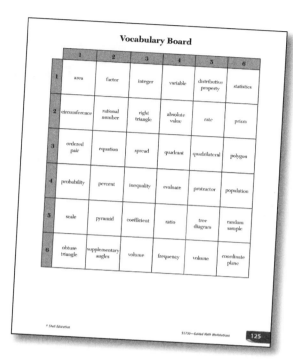

Describe connections to a math vocabulary word.

Materials

- *Vocabulary Board*
- *Making Connections* graphic organizer

Directions

1. Roll two number cubes and find the space where the row and column intersect. For example, a roll of 1 and 3 could be used as column 1 and row 3 (ordered pair) or column 3 and row 1 (integer).

2. Write your word or phrase in the space labeled Word on the *Making Connections* graphic organizer.

3. Think carefully about connections you have to the vocabulary word. Connections may be one of three types:

   - **My connections**—What personal connections do you have with the word?
   - **Math connections**—What other mathematical concepts have a connection to this vocabulary word?
   - **Real-world connections**—What does this mathematical concept look like in everyday life?

4. Complete the *Making Connections* graphic organizer. Remember to use precise mathematical language.

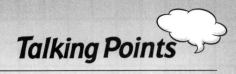

Talking Points

Vocabulary
• **connection**
• **reflect**
• **research**
• **discuss**
• **notice**
• **reason**

Talk like a mathematician:

The word _____ reminds me of _____ because _____.

I made a connection between _____ and _____ because _____.

This connection is important because _____.

I can relate the word _____ to _____ because _____.

- -

Talking Points

Vocabulary
• **connection**
• **reflect**
• **research**
• **discuss**
• **notice**
• **reason**

Talk like a mathematician:

The word _____ reminds me of _____ because _____.

I made a connection between _____ and _____ because _____.

This connection is important because _____.

I can relate the word _____ to _____ because _____.

Vocabulary Board

	1	2	3	4	5	6
1	area	factor	integer	variable	distributive property	statistics
2	circumference	rational number	right triangle	absolute value	rate	prism
3	ordered pair	equation	spread	quadrant	quadrilateral	polygon
4	probability	percent	inequality	evaluate	protractor	population
5	scale	pyramid	coefficient	ratio	tree diagram	random sample
6	obtuse triangle	supplementary angles	volume	frequency	volume	coordinate plane

Name: _____ Date: _____

Making Connections

Real-World

Math

My Connections

Word

51730—Guided Math Workstations   © *Shell Education*

Name: _____ Date: _____

Compare and Contrast

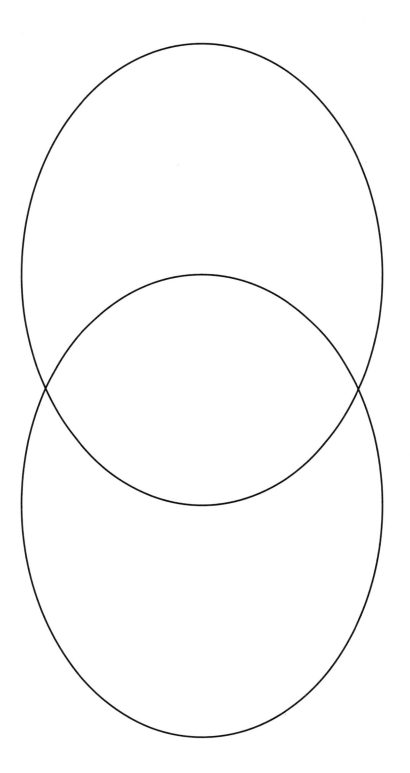

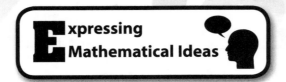

3-2-1 Learning Log

Overview

Reflection is an important part of synthesizing new learning. In addition, students need to be able to precisely communicate their mathematical thinking. This activity provides students a structured format to reflect on their learning of a current math topic.

Materials

- *3-2-1 Learning Log* (page 131)

- digital device for blogging (optional)

* The *Talking Points* card and these reproducibles are also provided in the Digital Resources (learninglogs.pdf)

Objective

Reflect on a math objective and precisely communicate mathematical thinking.

Procedure

1. Distribute copies of the *3-2-1 Learning Log* (page 131) and other materials to students. You may also have students use a variety of online tools to add choice and creativity to this task. If you have a class blog, have students write blog posts using the 3-2-1 format. This tool provides a great resource for parents to keep in touch with what is happening in the classroom.

2. Have students write three things they learned, two connections they made, and one question they still have.

Differentiation

- This task is self-differentiating since students will write at their own levels.

- Support **below-level learners** with sentence stems and frames.

3-2-1 Learning Log

Reflect on your learning of an important math concept.

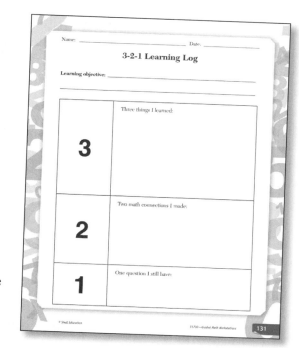

Materials

- *3-2-1 Learning Log*
- digital device for blogging (optional)

Directions

1. Write a learning objective. What is it that you are trying to master?

2. Write three things you have learned. What new learning do you have as a result of this unit of study?

3. Write two math connections you have made. How is this new learning connected to mathematical concepts you have previously studied?

4. Write one question you still have. What are you still wondering about or unsure of and how will you follow up?

5. Make sure you use precise mathematical language that clearly communicates your ideas.

Talking Points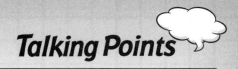

Vocabulary

- **connection**
- **reflect**
- **research**
- **pattern**
- **discuss**
- **notice**
- **reason**

Talk like a mathematician:

A pattern I noticed is _____.

I made a connection between _____ and _____ because _____.

I could learn more by _____.

_____ is important because _____.

_____ reminds me of _____ because _____.

I'm still not sure about _____ because _____.

Talking Points

Vocabulary

- **connection**
- **reflect**
- **research**
- **pattern**
- **discuss**
- **notice**
- **reason**

Talk like a mathematician:

A pattern I noticed is _____.

I made a connection between _____ and _____ because _____.

I could learn more by _____.

_____ is important because _____.

_____ reminds me of _____ because _____.

I'm still not sure about _____ because _____.

Name: _____ Date: _____

3-2-1 Learning Log

Learning objective: _____

_____

3	Three things I learned:
2	Two math connections I made:
1	One question I still have:

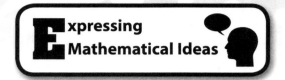

All About...

Overview

Students create a poster or digital presentation about a specific number or math topic.

Objective

Use precise mathematical language, numbers, and/or drawings to represent a mathematical concept.

Procedure

Note: This activity is purposefully unstructured to allow for a great deal of student choice and creativity. You may structure it as an activity to be completed in one class period, or you may allow students to stretch it into a longer project.

1. Distribute materials to students.

2. One option is for students to choose a number and represent that number in as many ways as possible. Students may create either posters or digital products, such as a digital slideshow presentations. Encourage students to include relevant math vocabulary, pictures representing the number, and real-world connections.

3. Another option is for students to create the same type of product using a math vocabulary term or topic, rather than a number. For example, students might choose *integers*, *ratios*, *angles*, or *functions*.

4. This type of activity allows students to use a wide variety of digital apps that are available to create a product, rather than just using digital apps to practice skills.

Differentiation

This activity adjusts easily for students of all levels. Offering students choices about the number or topic allows them to choose something within their comfort zone, yet still benefit from expressing their ideas using multiple representations.

All About…

Create a product to communicate everything you know about a number or a math vocabulary term.

Materials

- chart paper
- colored pencils or markers
- devices for taking photographs or videos and for creating a digital presentation (optional)

Directions

1. Choose a number and show everything you know about it using words, numbers, and pictures. Think about the following:

   - different ways to represent the number
   - examples in everyday life
   - personal connections
   - related vocabulary

2. Choose a vocabulary word or math topic and use words, numbers, and pictures to communicate everything you can about it. You might include the following:

   - meaning of the word in your own words
   - one or more pictures or drawings that represent the word
   - examples and non-examples
   - connections to everyday life
   - related math ideas

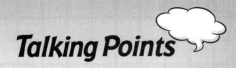

Vocabulary
• **plan**
• **goal**
• **justify**
• **represent**
• **connection**
• **notice**
• **observe**
• **diagram**
• **model**

Talk like a mathematician:

I made a connection between _____ and _____ because _____.

I can represent this number in multiple ways by _____.

This word reminds me of _____.

Clearly communicating my ideas is important because _____.

Talking Points

Vocabulary
• **plan**
• **goal**
• **justify**
• **represent**
• **connection**
• **notice**
• **observe**
• **diagram**
• **model**

Talk like a mathematician:

I made a connection between _____ and _____ because _____.

I can represent this number in multiple ways by _____.

This word reminds me of _____.

Clearly communicating my ideas is important because _____.

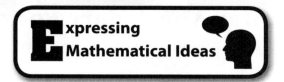

Expressing **M**athematical Ideas

Wanted Vocabulary Poster

Overview

Students create a wanted poster for a vocabulary term using words and pictures.

Materials

• *Wanted Poster* (page 138)

• colored pencils

• Math Word Wall or list of vocabulary terms

• *Dangerous Duo* (page 139)

* The *Talking Points* card and these reproducibles are also provided in the Digital Resources (poster.pdf)

Objectives

• Use precise language to communicate mathematical ideas.

• Make connections between related mathematical concepts.

Procedure

1. Distribute copies of the *Wanted Poster* (page 138) and other materials to students. You might assign the words or let students choose.

2. Students complete the *Wanted Poster* as follows:

   • **Name**: vocabulary term

   • **Description**: definition of term in students' own words

   • **Picture**: drawing showing vocabulary term

   • **Known Associates**: other vocabulary terms related to word

3. You may choose to collect and display students' posters.

Differentiation

• Support **below-level learners** by assigning them a vocabulary word that will help develop deeper understandings of a concept.

• **Above-level learners** may use the *Dangerous Duo* (page 139) to compare two vocabulary terms.

Wanted Vocabulary Poster

Create a Wanted poster describing a math vocabulary term using words and pictures.

Materials

- *Wanted Poster*
- colored pencils

Directions

1. Choose a vocabulary word. Think deeply about everything you know about this vocabulary word.

2. Complete your poster as follows:

   - **Name:** Write your vocabulary term.
   - **Description:** What does this term mean?
   - **Picture:** How can you illustrate this word?
   - **Known Associates:** What other mathematical ideas are connected to this word?

3. Remember to use precise mathematical language.

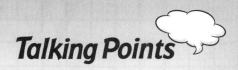

Talking Points

Vocabulary
• **model**
• **diagram**
• **pictorial representation**
• **connection**
• **precise**

Talk like a mathematician:

An example of _____ is _____ because _____.

My picture shows _____.

The most important thing about _____ is _____.

_____ is related to _____ because _____.

A non-example of _____ is _____ because _____.

I made a connection between _____ and _____ because _____.

✂ -

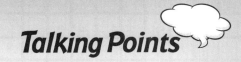

Talking Points

Vocabulary
• **model**
• **diagram**
• **pictorial representation**
• **connection**
• **precise**

Talk like a mathematician:

An example of _____ is _____ because _____.

My picture shows _____.

The most important thing about _____ is _____.

_____ is related to _____ because _____.

A non-example of _____ is _____ because _____.

I made a connection between _____ and _____ because _____.

WANTED

Name: _____

Description

_____

_____

_____

_____

_____

Picture

Known Associates

Dangerous Duo

Picture	Picture

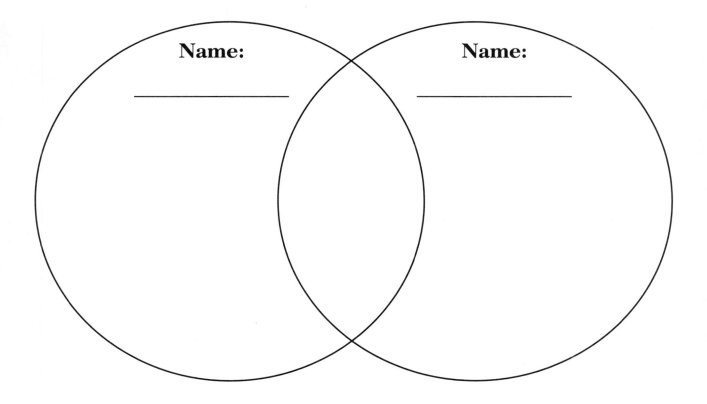

Name: _____

Name: _____

Appendix

References Cited

Diller, Debbie. 2011. *Math Work Stations: Independent Learning You Can Count On, K–2*. Portland: Stenhouse Publishers.

Sammons, Laney. 2010. *Guided Math: A Framework for Mathematics Instruction*. Huntington Beach: Shell Education.

————. 2013. *Strategies for Implementing Guided Math*. Huntington Beach: Shell Education.

————. 2014. *Guided Math Conferences*. Huntington Beach: Shell Education.

Answer Key

Fraction, Decimal, and Percent (page 19)

Fraction	Decimal	Percent
1/3	.33	33%
1/5	.20	20%
3/4	.75	75%
1/2	.50	50%
4/5	.80	80%
1/20	.05	5%

What's the Point? Cards (pages 47–50)

$6.25 \times 3.4 = 21.25$ $5.04 \times 15.9 = 80.136$ $5.8 \times 206.0 = 1194.8$ $235.2 \div 98 = 2.4$

$0.45 \times 12.3 = 5.535$ $60.2 \times 3.18 = 191.436$ $8.7 \times 2.48 = 21.576$ $50.85 \div 4.5 = 11.3$

$11.68 \times 2.4 = 28.032$ $30.3 \times 2.4 = 72.72$ $1.75 \times 60.2 = 105.35$ $6.656 \div 2.6 = 2.56$

$3.01 \times 17.5 = 52.675$ $5.6 \times 3.18 = 17.808$ $0.815 \times 2.04 = 1.6626$ $98.05 \div 5.3 = 18.5$

$0.37 \times 45.6 = 16.872$ $1.8 \times 145.0 = 261.0$ $7.65 \div 17 = 4.5$ $9.168 \div 0.24 = 38.2$

$22.3 \times 4.8 = 107.04$ $0.65 \times 120.0 = 78.0$ $15.77 \div 38 = 0.415$ $19.76 \div 6.5 = 3.04$

You Write the Story (page 59)

$m = \$8.75$ $c = 0.26$ $b = 15.4$ $a = 0.5$ $f = 12.9$ $t = 7$

Data Detective (page 79)

World Geography	
Mean	**Mode**
84.42	82
Median	**Range**
83	22

Cool Clothes Galore	
Mean	**Mode**
22.46	18
Median	**Range**
22.5	16

Bean Plants	
Mean	**Mode**
16.69	10, 22
Median	**Range**
16	20

Basketball Game	
Mean	**Mode**
43.5	4
Median	**Range**
41.5	18

Speed Limits	
Mean	**Mode**
25.44	25
Median	**Range**
25	11

Book Collections	
Mean	**Mode**
50.76	20
Median	**Range**
20	25

Fishing Tournament	
Mean	**Mode**
11.2	12
Median	**Range**
11.5	9

School Survey	
Mean	**Mode**
32.36	25, 45
Median	**Range**
30	25

Baseball Heart Rates	
Mean	**Mode**
66.88	60, 68, 70
Median	**Range**
68	26

Appendix

Rate and Ratio Task Cards (page 89)

1. Laura used 24 ounces of sugar.
2. The contractor will need 504 nails
3. It would cost $21.28 for 3 1/2 pounds of licorice mix.
4. Yummy Bakery sold 48 cups of coffee.
5. There are 336 insects for a total of 756 insects and spiders.
6. The pet store made $169.15 selling beta fish on Friday.
7. 24 jars will weigh 44.4 pounds.
8. Mrs. Lee bought 32 pens.
9. Jennifer ran 8.75 miles this week.
10. LaShawn should budget $84.50 for the gas on his trip.
11. The office building has 14 floors.
12. Nancy can make 9 bracelets with 135 beads.

GCF Bingo Cards (Game 1) (pages 97–98)

GCF of 27 and 6 = 3

GCF of 32 and 12 = 4

GCF of 42 and 28 = 14

GCF of 30 and 36 = 6

GCF of 56 and 24 = 8

GCF of 10 and 35 = 5

GCF of 35 and 14 = 7

GCF of 22 and 50 = 2

GCF of 72 and 63 = 9

GCF of 39 and 12 = 3

GCF of 57 and 21 = 3

GCF of 36 and 84 = 12

GCF of 18 and 48 = 6

GCF of 28 and 60 = 4

GCF Bingo (Game 2) (pages 99–100)

$3(9 + 2) = 27 + 6$

$4(8 + 3) = 32 + 12$

$14(3 + 2) = 42 + 28$

$6(5 + 6) = 30 + 36$

$8(7 + 3) = 56 + 24$

$5(2 + 7) = 10 + 35$

$7(5 + 2) = 35 + 14$

$2(11 + 25) = 22 + 50$

$9(8 + 7) = 72 + 63$

$3(13 + 4)\ 39 + 12$

$3(19 + 7) = 57 + 21$

$1(16 + 39) = 16 + 39$

$6(3 + 8) = 18 + 48$

$4(7 + 15) = 28 + 60$

$12(3 + 7) = 36 + 84$

Scientific Notation Task Cards (pages 113–116)

$2{,}300{,}000{,}000 = 2.3 \times 10^9$

$68{,}500{,}000 = 6.85 \times 10^7$

$500{,}000 = 5 \times 10^5$

$90{,}000{,}000 = 9 \times 10^7$

$37{,}000{,}000 = 3.7 \times 10^7$

$48{,}000{,}000{,}000 = 4.8 \times 10^{10}$

$705{,}000{,}000 = 7.05 \times 10^8$

$350{,}000{,}000 = 3.5 \times 10^8$

$0.000000345 = 3.45 \times 10^{-7}$

$0.0000701 = 7.01 \times 10^{-5}$

$0.00000067 = 6.7 \times 10^{-7}$

$0.000000314 = 3.14 \times 10^{-7}$

$0.000024 = 2.4 \times 10^{-5}$

$0.0006 = 6 \times 10^{-4}$

$0.0000005 = 5 \times 10^{-7}$

$0.0000098 = 9.8 \times 10^{-6}$

$3.8 \times 10^8 = 380{,}000{,}000$

$9 \times 10^6 = 9{,}000{,}000$

$8.55 \times 10^4 = 85{,}500$

$1.25 \times 10^5 = 125{,}000$

$2.06 \times 10^3 = 2{,}060$

$6.5 \times 10^5 = 650{,}000$

$1.4 \times 10^7 = 14{,}000{,}000$

$7.3 \times 10^6 = 7{,}300{,}000$

$5.8 \times 10^{-5} = 0.000058$

$2.03 \times 10^{-6} = 0.00000203$

$9.1 \times 10^{-7} = 0.00000091$

$8 \times 10^{-9} = 0.000000008$

$6.22 \times 10^{-4} = 0.000622$

$7 \times 10^{-3} = 0.007$

$1.75 \times 10^{-6} = 0.00000175$

$4.6 \times 10^{-7} = 0.00000046$

Digital Resources

Page(s)	Resource	Filename
16–19	Fraction, Decimal, and Percent Memory Game	memory.pdf
21–25	Difference from One	difference.pdf
27–31	Dodge the Zombie	angle.pdf
33–36	Integer Tug-of-War	tugofwar.pdf
38–39	Exploring Manipulatives	manipulatives.pdf
41–43	Cuisenaire® Rods Equations	equations.pdf
45–51	What's the Point?	point.pdf
53–55	Graphing Growing Patterns	patterns.pdf
57–61	You Write the Story	story.pdf
63–72	Express Yourself	express.pdf
74–79	Data Detective	detective.pdf
81–85	Slope and Intercept	slope.pdf
87–93	Rate and Ratio Task Cards	rate.pdf
95–105	Greatest Common Factor Bingo	bingo.pdf
107–110	Integer Battle	battle.pdf
112–121	Scientific Notation	scientific.pdf
123–127	Making Connections	connections.pdf
129–131	3-2-1 Learning Logs	learninglogs.pdf
133–134	All About…	allabout.pdf
136–137	Wanted Vocabulary Poster	poster.pdf
—	*Fraction Tiles*	fractiontiles.pdf

Notes